"The Object Les[...] [...] to magic: the b[...] [...] and animate th[...] [...] political struggle, science, and popular mythology. Filled with fascinating details and conveyed in sharp, accessible prose, the books make the everyday world come to life. Be warned: once you've read a few of these, you'll start walking around your house, picking up random objects, and musing aloud: 'I wonder what the story is behind this thing?'"

Steven Johnson, author of *Where Good Ideas Come From* and *How We Got to Now*

"Object Lessons describes themselves as 'short, beautiful books,' and to that, I'll say, amen. . . . If you read enough Object Lessons books, you'll fill your head with plenty of trivia to amaze and annoy your friends and loved ones—caution recommended on pontificating on the objects surrounding you. More importantly, though . . . they inspire us to take a second look at parts of the everyday that we've taken for granted. These are not so much lessons about the objects themselves, but opportunities for self-reflection and storytelling. They remind us that we are surrounded by a wondrous world, as long as we care to look."

John Warner, *The Chicago Tribune*

OBJECTLESSONS

A book series about the hidden lives of ordinary things.

Series Editors:

Ian Bogost and Christopher Schaberg

In association with

Program
in Public Scholarship

Washington
University in St. Louis

BOOKS IN THE SERIES

Pencil

CAROL BEGGY

BLOOMSBURY ACADEMIC
NEW YORK • LONDON • OXFORD • NEW DELHI • SYDNEY

BLOOMSBURY ACADEMIC
Bloomsbury Publishing Inc
1385 Broadway, New York, NY 10018, USA
50 Bedford Square, London, WC1B 3DP, UK
29 Earlsfort Terrace, Dublin 2, Ireland

BLOOMSBURY, BLOOMSBURY ACADEMIC and the Diana logo are trademarks
of Bloomsbury Publishing Plc

First published in the United States of America 2024

Cover design: Alice Marwick

Bloomsbury Publishing Inc does not have any control over, or responsibility for, any third-party
websites referred to or in this book. All internet addresses given in this book were correct at the
time of going to press. The author and publisher regret any inconvenience caused if addresses
have changed or sites have ceased to exist, but can accept no responsibility for any such changes.

Whilst every effort has been made to locate copyright holders the publishers would be grateful to
hear from any person(s) not here acknowledged.

Library of Congress Cataloging-in-Publication Data
Names: Beggy, Carol, author.
Title: Pencil / Carol Beggy.
Description: New York : Bloomsbury Academic, 2024. | Series: Object lessons | Includes
bibliographical references and index. | Summary: "Often overlooked, tucked into a drawer or
stuffed into a case, the pencil is a tool whose simplicity belies its usefulness and indeed, as a work
of design and technology that endures around the globe, its greatness"– Provided by publisher.
Identifiers: LCCN 2023031790 (print) | LCCN 2023031791 (ebook) | ISBN 9781501392245
(paperback) | ISBN 9781501392238 (epub) | ISBN 9781501392221 (pdf) | ISBN 9781501392214
Subjects: LCSH: Pencils.
Classification: LCC TS1268 .B44 2024 (print) | LCC TS1268 (ebook) | DDC 674/.88–dc23/
eng/20230822
LC record available at https://lccn.loc.gov/2023031790
LC ebook record available at https://lccn.loc.gov/2023031791

ISBN: PB: 978-1-5013-9224-5
ePDF: 978-1-5013-9222-1
eBook: 978-1-5013-9223-8

Series: Object Lessons

Typeset by Deanta Global Publishing Services, Chennai, India
Printed and bound in Great Britain

To find out more about our authors and books visit www.bloomsbury.com and sign up for our
newsletters.

For all those for whom a pencil is an object of
great affection—
and so much more.

CONTENTS

FIGURES

INTRODUCTION

As newly minted King Charles III signed a visitors' book at Hillsborough Castle in Belfast, Northern Ireland, on September 13, 2022, he realized that his pen was leaking and said "Oh God, I hate this thing!"[1] Charles then handed the inky mess to his wife, Queen Consort Camilla, who responded: "Oh look, it's everywhere." It was a rare mishap in an otherwise flawless week of events to honor the passing of the king's mother, Queen Elizabeth II. Charles, who has been photographed at well-appointed desks for decades, might want to reconsider his writing instrument. A pencil, rarely invited to such formal affairs, would never have let him down in such a public way.

I use pencils for writing. Artists use them to sketch, draw, shade, or just remember the shape of something. Engineers employ fancy calculators and other tools, but always have a pencil with a hard-grade core or lead handy. Librarians, particularly those working in special collections or with historical material, work almost exclusively in pencil. It is a communication tool that has been in regular use in roughly its current form for more than three hundred and fifty years.

Estimates say that two billion pencils are made worldwide every year. In other words, the humble pencil is not only useful, but still very much in use.

To love a pencil is to use it and to use it and use it. To sharpen it, draw with it, write with it is to destroy it as it wears down to a nub with a ragged eraser. (Pencils expect the errors we all make.) Yet, the pencil—an interior cylinder of baked graphite and clay, all housed in a wood case—creates as it is being destroyed.

Pencils are ubiquitous, perhaps because they are relatively inexpensive *and* a reliable tool (sharpeners help). You can buy a passable pencil for less than fifty cents, and you can find some marvelous pencils for less than a dollar. Those by United States-based makers include Musgrave's Test Scoring 100 or the Bugle and General's Cedar Pointe (particularly the No. 2) and the Badger. But I'm scribbling ahead of myself.

Even in an age when you can do almost anything easily on a mobile device, many people still opt to write things out by hand. One reason for the pencil's longevity is its classic functionality. A pencil has no battery to charge and it won't run out of ink or leak. The pencil works better than the pen despite (or maybe because of) its impermanence. With all the "mightier than the sword" stuff, you could argue that the pen has had a better PR campaign, and yet it can't write upside down, stops working in the cold, and has enough internal parts that it can readily break. When a pencil is broken in two, a quick sharpening sends it right back to the page.

"To reflect on the pencil is to reflect on engineering; a study of the pencil is the study of engineering," Henry Petroski, a Duke University professor and engineer, wrote in the preface of his groundbreaking work *The Pencil: A History of Design and Circumstance*.[2] He not only details the history of pencil-making but breaks down the process of its manufacture. I would pay to tour a pencil factory to watch pencils being made, and yet the complex forty-step process of making this deceptively simple-looking implement does not account for what people do with the pencil. The mystery of creativity that emerges from its tip is what I find fascinating.

The pencil and its echoes have penetrated everyday life and language in ways that other technology rarely does. You can pencil in a lunch meeting with a friend. There is the pencil skirt (narrow and straight), a pencil pusher (someone with a tedious clerical job), penciling something out (to tackle a problem in a rough draft), a pencil neck (a derogatory term for a weak person), the pencil tree (a Mediterranean cypress), pencil on (a once-popular term for an actor who is available for work), and the pencil cactus (a deceptively pleasant-looking plant that produces a poisonous latex).

Most of us used pencils, or certainly their colorful cousins the crayons, before any other communications device. They're just so common that we can forget how central they remain to us. Pencils have been used to sketch the greatest works of art. They were long a staple of democratic elections and are still used at the polls in the United Kingdom. (The UK Electoral Commission's media handbook issued for the

2017 election gives a long explanation that can be reduced to: we use pencils because that is tradition and because pencil marks are cleaner than ink, though using a pencil is not legally required.[3])

That notation captures the beauty of the pencil: it is utilitarian and trustworthy. Even when used to mark out where a saw's blade should make a cut (measure twice, cut once), the pencil is often overlooked and under-appreciated. (Try cutting that board without it and you're in for a frustrating day.) But the pencil is worthy of our notice.

If this wood-cased wonder hasn't always been considered fashionable in the strutting digital age, it is nonetheless experiencing a resurgence in interest with Facebook pages and groups, threads on Reddit that have spawned subreddits by the score, podcasts, and even brick-and-mortar stores dedicated to pencils (and its flashier cousin, the pen). Traditional media isn't rediscovering the pencil because it never really could quit it. Every autumn brings the return of schoolchildren and the reworking of the "best school supplies" stories. Some coverage goes even further like the *New York Times*'s *Wirecutter* blog post on October 15, 2020, wondering whether the iconic Dixon Ticonderoga yellow pencil is the "world's best."[4] Spoiler alert: no.

Writing with a pencil draws in our senses. The whirl of the old-fashioned, hand-crank sharpener or the zipping hum of an electric machine is unmistakable, particularly to schoolchildren. There is a subtle sound when the graphite meets the paper, sometimes scratchy, sometimes smooth. A pencil gives feedback in its strokes. The writing has a different feel from the plastic tapping of an electronic keyboard. For mathematicians and scientists, the pencil is still the first tool of choice to sort through a problem. The pencil, which requires swirling effort, can slow you down or allow you to speed up in mapping an outline. Some stationery fans even devote hours of study to the "toothiness" of paper brands in numerous notebooks. Looking for the perfect combo can seem like a Holy Grail quest, not that any paper nerds would complain about such.

Once sharpened, a pencil is constantly changing. Each stroke and every turn of a sharpener transforms it in size, clarity, and balance. Work a bit more, and then it is time to sharpen the pencil again. You have to sharpen a pencil (or change or shape the "lead") to keep it working as a hand tool, much the way chefs have to sharpen and hone their knives. There is a distinct smell of the pencil when sharpened, and pencils have a taste, even though writers have struggled to keep them out of their mouths as they puzzle problems. Some inveterate chewers could take their pencils to the dentist for an accurate bite check. The most obvious, of course, is the mark that pencils make, from light to dark depending on the pressure, the writer's hesitancy, or the "grade" of the pencil's core. (Note: There is no "lead" in pencils—the core is actually graphite.)

As a tool, a pencil can be tucked behind an ear, used to hold up long hair, munched on while thinking through a problem, sharpened to a sword point and meticulously lined up for classroom test taking (always No. 2s, the little black dress of pencils). They can prop up a weak plant stem or keep a door latch from fully locking. A pencil used to be the go-to tool for when a cassette tape needed to be rewound, but that seems like one too many analog references for even the proudest Luddite.

A pencil can even be used to tell time. Novelist John Steinbeck is said to have plowed through a minimum of two dozen pencils a day, all of which he had sharpened in the morning. He knew he had written enough when all of them were dulled, their essence turned into dynamic characters and dilemmas on the page.[5]

1 VARIATIONS ON A THEME

Without giving it much thought, I always seem to be able to pick the writing instrument that is best suited for the job at hand. A pencil when researching or outlining. A marker to make a note on a folder, or to write on an envelope or box. A pen for signing a document, always in blue ink to show that my signature is authentic. Other circumstances call for a keyboard, and there are still government agencies that only accept information by Fax.

The choice is often made for function, but it can be a deliberate selection of what feels good while trying to craft the perfect sentence or write the appropriate note. After a career of working as a reporter and editor for newspapers, I know that using whatever tool you have to get your story out as timely as possible is the correct tool to use. But when you have a moment to think about not just what you are writing but how you are doing it, using a pencil can be so much more than just making marks on paper.

Choosing the right pencil aids in the creation and enhances the writing process. A smooth first stroke on the paper, the act when those first words hit the page, is the moment for me that the writing process begins. This is when the pencil is more than a tool and more than an object—it is the precise point of creation. Or, as Betty Cornfield and Owen Edwards wrote in their 1983 book *Quintessence: The Quality of Having It*, pencils, specifically Eberhard Faber's Mongol No. 2, "are instruments of the mind's music."[1]

I have long envied the artist, who sketches, shades, darkens, erases, and then sketches a few strokes more to make art, where the very act of moving the pencil *is* the creative process. My jealousy dissipated after a conversation with an artist who worked *en plein air*. The artist moves quickly to capture the moment, I was told, in a whirlwind process where the work of art is produced outdoors, usually in one session. As a writer, the artist countered, I could return to my notes or thoughts of a particular point in time as much as I wanted. That is true for fiction, maybe even poetry, but I am dubious about that approach for journalism, which is the writing equivalent of *en plein air*; you must move fast and report on the scene in front of you. It could work for long-form narrative nonfiction.

It was while using a pencil (or five) to map out this chapter that I was reminded of something the late British novelist Hilary Mantel wrote in *The Guardian* about being too precious with the whole process. "Writers displace their anxiety on to the tools of the trade. It's better to say that you haven't got the right pencil than to say you can't write, or to blame your computer for losing your chapter than face up to your feeling that it's better lost. It's not just writers who muddle up the tools with the job. The reading public also fetishizes the kit."[2]

Still, what fun would it be if we didn't have a favorite pencil or a pen? As I worked on the manuscript for this book, my "kit" (confession: it really is *kits*) includes pencils, of course: a vintage Eagle Pencil Company's Black Warrior 372 in a No. 2 grade; a Derwent Graphic in HB; a Ryman-branded HB; a couple of Caran d'Ache editing duo-tone pencils, one red and graphite, the other red and blue; a "stub" of an editing pencil that comes in handy when researching in archives; a US-made Golden Bear; and a current production Blackwing Natural, along with a typewriter eraser that has a brush on the end (to clean the dust and crumbs out of my keyboard), a sharpener of some type, a few pens (usually a click pen or two that I've picked up at my bank), too many erasers (you never know what you might need to clean up), several highlighters, binder clips, a few brads (paper fasteners) and other office supplies. I almost always carry a Staedtler Wopex, a pencil made from 70 percent wood and the rest "polymers and additives," according to the packaging, that is "extruded" into a pencil shape. I do not know what that actually means, but a Wopex is practically impossible to sharpen without destroying the blade on your sharpener. It also is nearly indestructible and is handy for when you need to prop open a door or window or the hood of your car. And it writes! (fig. 1)

FIGURE 1 A pencil fanatic's "kit" is one part practical and three parts what we're feeling on a given day. Even the "thing" we carry our pencils in. Carol Beggy.

Where pencils fit in the office supplies pantheon probably depends on the user, but even stacking the sticks up against an IBM Selectric typewriter, I believe the pencil can hold its own. "Don't underestimate the pencil," renowned graphic artist Lou Brooks once told me. Brooks, who died in 2021 at the age of seventy-seven, is known for his work in transforming comic book art, redesigning the Monopoly board game logo, his many advertising campaigns for companies such as Coca-Cola, Budweiser, and Nikon, and having his artwork animated for television shows.[3] For me, however, he was at his best when he founded the Museum of Forgotten Art Supplies, an online, curated romp through the best of the tools used when the printed world hadn't yet become fully computerized.[4] I chatted with Brooks at an event some years ago in New York City and engaged him on the old, paste-up process for newspapers where each column of type was cut and pasted by hand. (Yes, using an X-Acto knife, we actually cut lines, sometimes single letters of type and pasted it on a page.) The conversation veered toward the editing process and he spoke up to defend the pencil as an editing tool. Later, I remembered that some people I know seek out pencils that were produced in the early 1990s featuring Brooks' *Comix* art. You can find unopened packages on eBay for about twenty-five dollars for five pencils. Not to be underestimated, indeed.

Much like golfers with many clubs in their bags, pencil users usually carry several pencils in a variety of grades—the darkness or lightness of the mark made by the core when the pencil is used. If the user is an artist or a teacher, the array of pencils in use could more than double, with containers and rollable carriers full of colored pencils and every grade and shade of graphite.

The Germany-based Faber-Castell company has a helpful online guide for understanding pencil "lead" grades, which runs from the softest and darkest core (more graphite and less clay) to hardest and lightest cores (less graphite and more clay.)[5] Most writers stick to the middle of the range with a B (soft black), HB (hard black), F (fine) and H (hard) among the primary choices. In pencil circles, the comparable grades to US-made pencils are much debated, with the HB mostly lining up to the No. 2 that American pencil users have come to know. The consistency of HB pencils made by Faber-Castell, which was founded in 1761 and is the world's oldest pencil manufacturer, is unquestioned. The likelihood that Faber-Castell's pencil with an HB core is exactly as that made by rival maker Koh-i-Noor is uncertain. The cores are made through a mix of the mineral graphite, the crystalline form of carbon, with clay, but each maker's formula is unique. And, that recipe for each company is a heavily guarded secret, right up there with what is actually in McDonald's "secret sauce" or which eleven herbs and spices the Colonel uses.

There is no standard measure of pencil grades or variations out there. Like different models of cars, pencils all do the same basic thing: they make marks on a surface but offer different features. Pencils are all roughly seven-

and-a-half inches long, with a graphite or color core that is housed in a case, most often made of wood. They come in the standard hexagonal—or "hex"—shaped barrel, though they can be round or sometimes triangular. I own a couple of five-sided pencils, a few square pencils, and even a heart-shaped pencil. There is a vintage Bookmark pencil from the Eagle Pencil Co. that was made flat enough to fit inside your book. But there are a lot of other "pencil" types. Once, when I had cobbled together enough miles and segments, I flew from Los Angeles to Boston on American Airlines in First Class and was seating next to a chatty CEO, who, after the initial introductions, said: "Tell me something I don't know." I asked if he knew anything about pencils and then started my impromptu lecture on all things pencil.

Occasionally, he would stop me to ask a question. "How do you define a pencil?" He clarified that he wanted to know if I thought that mechanical pencils are "pencils." Of course, they are. As are bullet pencils that take their name from the bullet casings that were used to house the graphite core. Soldiers would use spent casings to house a stick of graphite. For those soldiers in the field in the Civil War, it was often the only way to write a letter. Ink and dip pen are not handy in such situations. Later bullet pencils often featured advertising on the metal body that held the pencil stub and were promoted as convenient for carrying in your pocket.[6] The modern equivalent became a popular advertising and promotion for businesses, mostly in the US Midwestern states.

I later checked one of my dictionaries—pencil nerds tend to be the type of people who have more than one printed dictionary to check for original meanings—the *Webster's Collegiate Dictionary* (fifth edition) that was printed in 1948. My mom won this much-loved book while in junior high at St. Lawrence O'Toole parish in the Garfield neighborhood of Pittsburgh, Pennsylvania. Yes, I knew what a pencil is, but not everyone agrees. That dictionary has the object of this book as its third definition, "a slender cylinder or strip of black lead, colored chalk, etc., usually encased in wood, for writing or drawing."[7] (The current edition of that dictionary, also available online, is the reference for this series.)

Fittingly, there are innumerable variations on office pencils such as those that were made for stenographers (a person whose job it is to transcribe speech, as is done in courtrooms) with sharpened points on both ends to ensure that you would not have to stop because of a broken point. Some pencils have erasers that are very thin so that a mistake can be erased while a document is still in the typewriter. There are others that write so dark that they fill in imperfections on film, "non-repo blue" pencils where the writing cannot be seen by photocopiers or cameras, and pencils with yellow cores where the writing can be seen on architectural plans.

My conversation with the CEO included some questions about whether US pencil makers were better than the European ones and whether the quality was worth the cost. After a short discussion about how China cranks out millions of cheap pencils with little regard for quality or consistency, I told him how the United States, Japanese, Portuguese, Indian, Czech, and German manufacturers produce high-quality pencils in a multitude of varieties. One example I used was that Faber-Castell sells "The Perfect Pencil" with a pencil and a plastic cover/extender that has an integrated sharpener. (They offer several price points: about thirteen US dollars for one with a green plastic cap, a forty-nine-dollar version with a metal cover, and a specialty line of Graf von Faber-Castell editions in platinum and silver finishes that top three hundred dollars.) I added with a bit of sarcasm that only a German engineer would call his creation the "perfect" one, but it is a pretty good line of products. I regularly use the cheaper models. You have to keep an eye on such pencils, I told the CEO; they tend to be "borrowed." As we got off the plane and headed back to the terminal, the CEO asked me, "Hey, can I borrow a pencil?" I reached into my backpack and gave him my used Perfect Pencil, with a green plastic cover.

* * *

I want to be nice. I do. When you ask me if you can borrow my pencil, I want to hand it over. Truth is that I almost always pause and do a quick mental inventory to determine what other pencils I might have with me. I will lend you a pencil, but it's unlikely that I'll give you the pencil that I am currently using. I probably just got it to the length that I like, the length that fits perfectly in my right hand, my writing hand. The hand that still has a writer's callus, even though I no longer write exclusively with a pen or pencil for hours at a time. So, no. No way am I handing over this pencil, but I will give you a pencil.

I *will* give my mom the pencil I am using so that she can finish her Sudoku puzzle. I am not a barbarian.

I have met some pencil fanatics who will carry pencils they don't care about (maybe a cheaper pencil, something made in China, a brand they don't like to use, see also "Wopex") for sharing or lending. There are others who are like Johnny Appleseed only doling out the best pencils, the kind they seek out and pay extra for like the modern era Blackwing, a Uni Mitsubishi 9000 (in an HB grade for me, thank you), a Camel with an eraser cap, or any of the Viarco 3000 No. 2s. They believe that sharing a crappy pencil is a crappy thing to do. They are good people.

2 MAKING THEIR MARK

Even savvy business leaders seem surprised when you answer "Yes!" to the question: "Are pencils still made in the United States?" Any aficionado can run through the lineup of what's made where without much difficulty, at least that's been my experience. You are here forewarned about asking this question of a pencil person. You are not engaging in small talk. It still seems to matter to US-based and international users and collectors alike where their pencils are made and by what company. There is a nostalgia for both vintage brands and current US-made models. So here goes.

There is the General Pencil Company, Jersey City, NJ, where pencils are made by the thousands in a beautiful process that photographer Christopher Payne captured for a 2018 photo essay for the *New York Times Magazine*.[1] In his images you see not only the beauty of the pencils and the workers making them, but the sometimes dirty and very industrial process of producing pencils. Tourists who find themselves in Jersey City usually head toward Liberty State

Park for the sweeping views of the Statue of Liberty, Ellis Island, and the Manhattan skyline. Me? I did a drive-by of General's Fleet Street factory.

General Pencil is a privately-owned business, run by the Weissenborn family since 1889 and now overseen by James Weissenborn and his daughter Katie.[2] They make many high-quality pencils, including a favorite of mine, the Cedar Pointe #333 2HB, an inexpensive pencil in a natural finish (no coats of paint) with black lettering, a black eraser and ferrule (that's the metal band that secures the eraser to the pencil). General also makes the dark-writing Layout No. 555 that is a go-to for graphic designers, engineers, and editors, and the Test Scoring 580, a great choice for, you guessed it, taking tests or filling out forms that will be scanned. But the stars of the show are the range of yellow pencils with whimsical names: Badger, Goddess, Pacific, and Semi-Hex, which is a nod to the shape of the pencil. The latter is six-sided without a hard edge so it's easy on your hand. I cannot overlook General's many pencils for visual artists that include Kimberly watercolor pencils, charcoal pencils, and a range of drawing pencils that have grades from 9H (the hardest and lightest) to the Kimberly 525 9XXB that puts down a mark so dark you might think it was written with a Sharpie marker.

Another manufacturer, Moon Products of Lewisburg, Tennessee, was formerly J.R. Moon Pencil Company, which was founded in 1961 by a group that included James R. Moon, the company's first president. (He had previously worked for the Linton Pencil Company and the American Pencil Company.[3]) The company still has a few pencils that carry a product name, the best-known of which is the Try-Rex, a triangular-shaped, oversized pencil that is favored by kindergarten teachers as the first pencil used by tiny hands.

The Musgrave Pencil Company is family-owned and operates out of Shelbyville, TN, which was dubbed "Pencil City, USA," because a half dozen manufacturers once had factories in the Middle Tennessee town. I will admit that I have a soft spot for Musgrave pencils. They have many "brand name" offerings, what we pencil geeks call the various offerings like a make of a car or a different style of sneaker. I know that some people find using the Musgrave pencils with a "hard hex" uncomfortable because of the sharply defined edges, but it makes for a clean-looking pencil. By the way, that's not the weirdest thing I've heard from users over the years, some of whom do not like round pencils or pencils that have an eraser because it shifts the weight while you are writing or drawing. If you haven't noticed by now, pencil people think about everything related to the pencil. *Everything*.

Musgrave is run by Henry Hulan whose grandfather James "The Colonel" Raford Musgrave founded the company in 1916.[4] I have wondered if the Musgrave Bugle 1816 No. 2 with two bugle icons on each pencil might have been a reference to the Colonel. But this amazing stick doesn't need a backstory. The Bugle also comes in a variation with a half-natural and half-black finish that, when sharpened, creates some pretty jazzy duo-toned shavings. There's a 600 News that

I first saw being used at a newspaper's Display Desk, which is a fancy name for the people who placed the advertisements on the pages; the silver-barreled Test Scoring 100 that has a logo that includes squares that look like an answer sheet; and, the Choo-Choo 8500, which is an oversized yellow pencil with an old-fashioned train engine and tender emblazoned in blue ink. Musgrave, too, sells yellow pencils of all grades and an artist-centric line of Unigraph 1200 with multiple grades. But the real show-stopper is the Musgrave Single Barrel 106, which is made from a trove of vintage Tennessee red cedar found in the company's warehouse. The pencil has the shocking (to some) price of ten dollars each, nine if you buy the two-pack, and is finished so that the deep wood grain, unique to each pencil, shines through. Compared to the price of a top-line pen? Ten dollars is a steal.

And then there's the Dixon company. Perhaps no US pencil is as easily identifiable as the Dixon Ticonderoga, with its green ferrule with two yellow stripes atop a bright yellow body. The pencil has been a mainstay in US schools for decades. Trouble is, the Ticonderoga is and *isn't* a US pencil. The company has a long and rich history that mirrors the growth of the United States. Joseph Dixon (1799-1869) founded his crucible company in Massachusetts and later moved to Jersey City, NJ, where the company made pencils by the millions before closing the plant in the 1980s.[5] The Dixon company has long dominated the school market with its "penny pencils" in the 1920s and its Cabinet pencils, a high-end brand of dark wood pencils that were used in offices, and several pencils with fancy paint and oversized and unusually shaped ferrules. For decades, the plant cranked out more than 130 pencils every minute, a technological advance for which Dixon received a patent in 1866.[6]

Eventually, Dixon decamped from Northern New Jersey; its site is now the Dixon Mills apartment complex, and the company started to become a more international operation. You might need a Harvard MBA to figure out the company's actual home today. Owned by FILA, an Italian art supply conglomerate with factories in twenty-two countries, Dixon's US headquarters is in Appleton, Wisconsin, but Dixon does not make graphite pencils in the United States anymore. This has been the subject of debates including in Washington, DC, where lawmakers have granted Dixon trade protections and federal funds to fend off the dumping of millions of cheaper China-made pencils, according to a 2018 story in the *Washington Post*.[6] That bit of tarnish on the Dixon reputation does nothing to stop its fans from seeking out its brand. If you should ever find a box of Dixon pencils with a "USA" stamped on them, or even a box of black Ticonderogas made in Mexico, I know dozens of people who would gladly pay you for them.

Several foreign manufacturers have offices in the United States, such as Faber-Castell's plant in Cleveland, Ohio, and Koh-I-Nor of the Czech Republic's operations in Leeds, Massachusetts. The US pencils companies have always had connections to their European antecedents, a fact of both pride and even concern as was the case for Eberhard

Faber, makers of the spectacularly versatile Van Dyke and the vaunted original Blackwing. (An explanation: The Blackwing 602, which it's distinctive, flattened ferrule, was made by Eberhard Faber until the 1980s, and then it was made by other companies. A modern version is produced by California Cedar Products Company. If you need proof of the Blackwing 602's importance in the pencil world, you can consult its Wikipedia page.[7]) Eberhard Faber, which was started by a wing of the same family that created what is now Faber-Castell, was so concerned about its German heritage during World War I that it took out full-page ads in daily newspapers across the country on October 18, 1918, professing its American-ness. "Every member of the firm of Eberhard Faber is a native-born American citizen, true to the principles of his citizenship," said the ad, printed about a year and a half after the United States entered the war. "We ask you to get it firmly in mind that every Eberhard Faber product, be it lead pencil, eraser, pen holder or rubber band, is solely and purely American."[8] The big concern then was that US companies might have been importing things like graphite, rubber for erasers, or varnish for finishes from countries that were now enemies and supporting their economies.

Like so many who have gone down the pencil rabbit hole, I started with retired Duke University engineering professor Henry Petroski's 1990 definitive and expansive tome *The Pencil, A History of Design and Circumstances*, which details the world history of pencils, the making of pencils (he's an engineer after all), and the many brands and uses. Before that, Pulitzer Prize-winning reporter William Ecenbarger wrote a 1985 story for the *Philadelphia Inquirer* that is the first modern history of Eberhard Faber and other US brands, how they were used, and by whom. Numerous stories in the decades since have used Ecenbarger's reporting, often without attribution. I won't make that mistake. From his "lede" paragraph:

> Consider the pencil. The ubiquitous, yellow (primarily), 7-inch, 2-for-a-quarter lead pencil—the simplest, most convenient, least expensive of all writing instruments. The most useful, least appreciated, most stolen article in the world. Servant of poet and banker alike, mightier than the pen or the sword. [. . .] The pencil is, perhaps, humanity's closest approach to perfection.[9]

I had an actual newspaper clipping of Ecenbarger's piece put in my hand by a former *Boston Globe* colleague and found it later on microfilm. The task of research, particularly for hobbyists, got easier when Newspapers.com offered hundreds of editions dating back 200 years. Ecenberger was writing when there were still seventeen American pencil companies producing about 1.9 billion pencils a year, and pencils were still the tool of choice in most government offices, which produced a lot of forms. [10]

The knowledge started to flow with the advent of the Internet and one of the earliest websites for pencil fans was The Pencil Pages (pencilpages.com) created and edited by

Doug Martin, who, among his many notable titles, was the editor of the American Pencil Collectors Society's newsletter, *The Pencil Collector*. I know a lot about pencils, but I do not consider myself an expert; I am a fan whose professional life trained her to find great stories and research history. Doug is an expert in all things related to brand name pencils and the US history of collecting. Doug and that newsletter are where I learned all about the many US pencil makers, the different types of ferrules, and how to store my collection. I'm not the only one. Pencil Pages has been quoted in museum archives and even made an appearance in the 2015 documentary, *No. 2: The Story of the Pencil*.

It was in the online archives that I found an article in the *Cawker City Public Record*, a long-defunct Kansas newspaper, from December 23, 1886, that lists in great detail how a pencil is made. I think the date of publication probably allowed for such a long article because Christmas week is usually a slow time, news-wise. From the article: "The powder is lusterless and a dingy color. [. . .] The leads are now ready for their wooden case. For the cheapest pencil pine is used, for the common grades an ordinary quality of red cedar. [. . .] Filling the leads is done by girls, sitting at brass-covered tables."[11] I probably could not have found that piece if the only place it lived was in some dusty bound volumes in a Kansas archive, so I'm thankful for the technology assist in my research.

The pencil's origin story is not as easy to pin down as you might think. Most modern histories set the pencil's birth to the early sixteenth century in Keswick, Cumbria, in the United

Kingdom, when a "violent storm" knocked down a stand of trees and uprooted a deposit of pure graphite, also called plumbago.[12] Keswick is where the Derwent pencil company has its museum. Others say it was nearby Borrowdale, also in the Lakes Region, that was the source of this precious mineral that brought a high price to the mine owners.[13] Some say that pencil as we know it today was created by the French painter Nicolas-Jacques Conté, and others note that the first depictions of a pencil were made by Swiss naturalist Conrad Gessner in 1565. Still others point out that monks wrapped pieces of graphite in cloth or wood to make pencils.[14] I am thankful for all of them and their innovations.

The newspapers and websites also offer a look at the pencil manufacturers and the families behind them. As I was wrapping up the research on this book, I spoke with a fellow pencil fan in the United Kingdom about much of this history and when we came to the now-late Eberhard Faber company we both laughed. With an origin story of German immigrants who make their way to the United States and start making pencils on land that is now the United Nations, you already have the makings of a great historical novel. Add in the leaders of the company who died young under mysterious circumstances, and that a member of the European wing married into royalty, and you have the makings of a cable television series à la *Game of Thrones* meets *Succession*.

3 TOOLS OF THE TRADE

I was lucky enough to work in the newsroom of the *Boston Globe* while still a college student in the early 1980s. We did a lot of running around, answering telephones, and research in a library that had stacks upon stacks of bound editions of newspapers, clippings of articles in overstuffed brown folders, and thousands of printed photographs. It may sound heartless and it was never really talked about, but the one thing all young reporters hoped for was that enough "bad stuff" would happen that they got the call to cover some incident that might merit a small story in the morning edition. When you work in daily journalism, often someone's worst day is a "good" day for you—at least professionally.

One Saturday night, Metro Editor John C. Burke assigned me to go out to a multiple-alarm fire in East Boston, a neighborhood known for dangerous fires because of how close the houses are stacked together; back then, they were often covered in asphalt siding, too. Burke, an old-school newspaperman who always kept a few Dixon Ticonderoga pencils with long points on his desk and one tucked behind his ear, used to tell all the new reporters to take certain writing implements with them on their assignments. Your reporter rig could include whatever style of notebook you liked, a tape recorder and extra batteries, but it had to have a ballpoint pen, a felt-tipped pen, and a pencil. In a newsroom version of rock, paper, scissors, this trio would keep you working. A ballpoint pen writes fast but won't work in extreme cold and stops working if you start to write upside down. A felt-tip marker-style pen will write in extreme cold, but the ink smudges in rain or snow (or the misty blow-back of a firefighter's hose). The pencil might be inelegant and scratchy and the point may break in certain situations, but you can take notes with it, even if it is broken. A pencil is like a starfish: the more pieces you have the more potential pencils you have.

I have used this setup of pen, pencil, and marker on local assignments, countless meetings and press conferences, red carpet events such as the Academy Awards, and disasters around the United States, and it has never failed me. When all else gives out, including cell phone service and your battery, this combo will come through. A photographer friend added that his mentors also always carried a China Marker, sometimes called a grease pencil, made from a crayon-like wax that is "sharpened" by pulling a string to expose the core. A China Marker can write on nearly any surface, including a metal roll of film or, in more recent times, a disk from a camera. (fig. 2)

It is worth stopping for a moment to recognize the now all-too-rare office supply cabinet. The cabinets for supplies in the *Globe*'s newsroom of the 1980s filled an exterior wall in the heart of the newsroom. One was at least six-feet tall and had double, vertical hung doors with shelves filled with boxes of staplers and staples (in a variety of sizes), more than one type of scissors, several offerings of paper clips and other fasteners, tablets (most made in the company's in-house "job shop"), dozens of boxes holding a dozen pencils each, and pens, both plastic stick versions with erasers and colorful click pens with *Boston Globe* printed on them from the Hub Pen Company in Braintree, Massachusetts. There was another cabinet that was a double-wide stack of horizontal drawers filled with notebooks of all types from legal pads to steno-pads (a 6- by 9-inch notebook with a metal spiral binding on top) and reporter's notebooks, along with envelopes and company letterhead in several sizes. Special stationery and supply requests were welcomed and it was a student's job to deliver the supplies to the various offices and bureaus tucked into courthouses and government buildings in Eastern Massachusetts.

My connection with newspapers and pencils goes back to my childhood. My Pap-Pap, my mom's father, worked as a photoengraver, a production job that was usually "downstairs" from the news-gathering jobs "upstairs." Once, when I was about six years old, my Pap took me to work with him and introduced me to Cy Hungerford, the editorial cartoonist for the *Pittsburgh Post-Gazette*. My Pap prepped the editorial cartoons for printing so he knew the artist well, and he and

FIGURE 2 Whether in the office or in the field, the writers, editors and cartoonists at newspapers of yore used a variety of pencils. Richard "Moco" Yardley favored a Blaisdell. Reporters often carried a pencil, a ballpoint pen and a felt-tip marker. Carol Beggy.

Hungerford shared a love of the city's Duquesne Incline, an 800-foot railway that climbs the hill on Pittsburgh's South Side. When Hungerford championed efforts to save and rehab the funicular, my Pap and his production department colleagues helped make the posters and items in support of the project. Our visit was related to that extracurricular work (when the Incline got historic landmark status), and what I most remember about Hungerford's office was the way he hunched over his table, and that he had so many eraser-less pencils in his office.

Some years later, I met the daughter of the *Baltimore Sun* editorial cartoonist Richard "Moco" Yardley, who was friendly with Hungerford and other fellow artists creating editorial content in the mid-twentieth century. At some point in learning about her father's work and the many subjects Yardley took on, I asked her about his work setup. She said that her father had an office filled with the traditional tools of cartoonists (inks, fountain pens and nibs, paper and boards, and lots of pencils) and that he had his drawings and newspapers stacked around.

Yardley's favorite instrument to draw with was the Blaisdell 616-T, a wonder of engineering and pencil-making, that has a thick, dark, very soft, almost buttery core that is "sharpened" by pulling on a string to expose more of a point. While reading newspapers and listening to the radio, Yardley would use the Blaisdell to quickly sketch out ideas on big squares of cheap newsprint that were cut for him by the pressroom. He also used blue pencils for the under-drawings that were later inked. And, he used Eagle's Draughting model No. 314 that was advertised as "Chemi-Sealed," which is a fancy way of explaining how the wood slats of the pencil were secured together. Today there are online debates that rage on about which, if any, pencils still in production might replicate that wonderful old pencil and others. To my hand and eye, the modern pencil that most matches it is General's Draughting pencil, which is not "Chemi-Sealed," but does sport the No. G314, an apparent hat tip by the former competitor of Eagle. General also makes a "jumbo" (that's a pencil with a wider-girth body) in an HB/No. 2 that it calls the Cartooning pencil. They take their connections to artists seriously.

Pencils have always been a part of the periodical writer's arsenal. A search of the Boston Public Library's online holdings produced an electronic copy of an Irish publication from 1771 that lists as its author: "Written by a Gentleman of the *World*, who when he sat with certain People, *mentioned* and not *mentioned* in this Book, had always a Pencil and *Pocket-Book* about him."[1] (Emphasis supplied.)

Would that it was just a matter of having "a pencil in his pocket" and a notebook for great reporting to happen, but I have found a few principles that do help. My guidelines are:

1.) Clever never ends well. (Imprinted on me by my Gram Beggy.)

2.) When something doesn't make any sense, it's personal. (Taken from my former colleague Rus Lodi and modified.)

3.) There are no coincidences. (Quoted by just about everyone who ever worked as a newspaper editor.)

4.) And, sometimes paranoia is just a heightened sense of reality. (Totally lifted from my friend Bruce, who, I'm sure, lifted it from someone else.)

For me, that path to journalism started with a visit to a newspaper, meeting a legendary cartoonist, and having a paper route, which I split with James Smithhammer, who in those years I called Jimmy.

His family lived catty-corner from me on Lincoln Avenue in the part of Edgewood, Pennsylvania, that is bordered on one side by the Edgewood Towne Center shopping plaza and professional office building where my mom's doctor is (the old Union Switch & Signal) and the Norfolk Southern Railway and the two-lane, bus-only Martin Luther King, Jr. East Busway that takes commuters directly to downtown Pittsburgh, made from the ribbons of the old Pennsylvania Railroad line.

Right across from those tracks, just about a half a block from the house I grew up in, sits the C.C. Mellor Memorial Library at One Pennwood Avenue, and where this all came together for me. The library, where I got my first card when I was about six and could write my full name, is not very large and then occupied the second floor of a distinctive mission-style building that is also home to the Edgewood Club, a private club with swimming and courts for tennis, pickleball and bocce, and a large room that can be rented for weddings.

(It has since swapped out the bowling lanes for a children's section.) The building was a gathering spot for many events in the first eighteen years of my life, but it was the library that was the real draw.

My earliest years of library visits coincided with a librarian named Mr. Schroeder. He was a bespectacled man with wild wisps of hair, who would shush kids by simply putting his forefinger up to his lips and letting out a hiss that sounded like air coming out of a tire. I could not remember (and am not sure I ever really knew) his first name so I asked Jimmy, who answered without hesitation, "Alvin." I put the question to the current library staff, others in the community, and even posted in a borough-focused Facebook group, but I should have just trusted Jimmy. Not many were sure of his first name, but everyone had a story to share about Mr. Schroeder: how he remembered what books a family member had already checked out, that he let us read newspapers (as long as we put them back appropriately), and that he encouraged children to read by giving us prizes, although no one could remember what the treasures were.

Mr. Schroeder, like so many librarians, even those working today, used pencils. I remember his writing: he had impeccable printing and a cursive that I have since been told is called "library hand," a rounded style that was taught in library schools. Mr. Schroeder's pencils were sharpened to a dangerously fine point and always had erasers, and his pencils were tricked out with a special miniature stamp to record the date your books were due. This stamp was fastened by a clip onto the pencil allowing him to move quickly through the check-out process. I searched for years to learn more about the stamp and finally found a library history blog written by retired librarian Larry T. Nix. That magic stamp had a name—a "pencil dater"—and Nix had found an image and sales listing in a catalog for the Library Bureau, a company founded by Melvil Dewey, an educator and the inventor of the library classification Dewey Decimal system.[2] In the 1886 catalog, the pencil dater, with a complete set of date stamps, was sold for seventy-five cents and the listing noted it was "devised" at the Milwaukee (Wisconsin) Public Library. Nearly a century later, the pencil dater was still very much in use in libraries, and then it seemed to just go out of use and there is no record of why. (fig. 3)

That made me think of another place where pencils were in heavy use only to fall out of favor: the New York Stock Exchange. In 1991, the NYSE used 1 million pencils, according to an article by Ecenbarger in the *Baltimore Sun*.[3] A quick calculation puts that at nearly 4,000 pencils each day that the market was open. In those days, all transactions took place "after the morning bell" (there was no 24-hour trading) and brokers wrote out the tickets by hand on the floor of the Exchange. The scene, now relegated to old movies and historical photographs, was one of a well-choreographed chaos, with brokers yelling and men standing with a pencil or pen behind an ear, a stack of trade tickets in their hands.

Pencils are not used much, if at all, on the financial exchanges today, but when did it stop? I reached out to

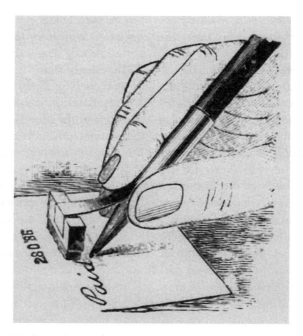

FIGURE 3 Melvil Dewey's wonderful invention, the "pencil dater," image taken from a catalog. Used with permission. https://heritage.wisconsinlibraries.org/entry/milwaukee-pencil-dater/

some "financial types" that I know, some of whom I have interviewed for important news stories, and none would go on the record about pencils at the stock exchange.

What I have been able to piece together, at least anecdotally, is that pencils were used in smaller and smaller numbers until the earliest days of the twenty-first century. Office supplies were not as ubiquitous as they once were, except for boxes of inexpensive ballpoint pens, my sources said. Trading was done, and news about business trends, individual stocks, and pending offerings came through terminals and electronic devices. This evolution took place gradually over decades but became obvious at the turn of the century. When asked about the moment when they no longer saw things like pencils around, my sources pointed to the tragic, deadly attack on the World Trade Center in lower Manhattan on September 11, 2001. When the NYSE reopened seven days later, the stock exchange, along with the city, the country, and much of the world was forever changed. "A lot of things did not come back the same," I was told by someone who worked on the floor of the NYSE. "We didn't come into work the way we did before, we didn't do our jobs as we had . . . all the old things had changed. They had to."

4 PEOPLE AND THEIR PENCILS

While paying tribute to the late Stephen Sondheim at the 2022 Tony Awards, Lin-Manuel Miranda was just a couple of sentences into his mini-eulogy when he showed just how well he knew the legendary Broadway composer.

"Steve touched our lives in a multitude of ways through his immortal music and lyrics, through his teaching and advocacy for young writers and through letters," said Miranda, a Tony and Grammy Award-winning composer, lyricist, and actor. "Stephen wrote them to friends, to up-and-coming artists, to countless people he'd never met. He wrote so many letters that you'd wonder when he had time to pick up a Blackwing 602 pencil and write a song. I stand here on behalf of generations of artists he took the time to encourage."[1]

What Miranda shared with the world is something we pencil fans already knew; Sondheim was gaga over the original Eberhard Faber Blackwing 602. So much so that he was reported to have stockpiled the pencil when the brand was discontinued in 1998.

Like a lot of musicians, Sondheim favored the Blackwing because its flattened ferrule, with a rectangular replaceable eraser, prevented the pencil from rolling off of piano tops or music stands. In explaining his process to D.T. Max of the *New Yorker* in a piece that ran in February 2022, about four months after Sondheim died, he said: "Yeah. What happens is, I write them out in pencil, like so. Then it goes to the copyist."[2]

For Sondheim, it didn't stop with pencils as he also had a preference for what he wrote on: yellow, lined pads which showed the contrast of the graphite better than white paper. In a 2005 interview, Sondheim detailed just how much he thought about his tools. "I used to have them, so it was, I think twenty-six lines to a page, and my friend, Burt Shevelove, who was a stationery freak, said, 'Buy cartons of them!' I said, 'Oh Burt, come on. I'll buy twelve pads. That will be enough.' God, was he ever right because they discontinued making them about twenty years ago," Sondheim said.

"I'm used to the other pads now. You get used to the exact amount of space between lines, because you write a word and then you write an alternate word over it. You want enough room so you can read it, so the lines can't be too close," he said, "but if they're too far apart, you don't get enough lines on the paper. I could go on. I'm sure many writers have these tiny little habits. All over the United States, there are people who only use Blackwings. I sometimes get letters, 'Do you have any source for the Blackwings?'"[3]

As you can tell from Sondheim's anecdote, the original Blackwing 602, with "Half the Pressure, Twice the Speed," imprinted on the barrel and its distinctive ferrule, stood out. "It's probably the most iconic pencil ever made in America," said Caroline Weaver, the author of two books on pencils and owner of the now-closed CW Pencil Enterprise shop in New York City, which she ran for more than seven years.[4] (The Blackwing was reborn in 2012 when California Cedar Products Company launched its version of the Blackwing under its Palomino brand that revived the distinctive flat ferrule.)

The Blackwing was famous for all its famous users: Walt Disney and Disney Studios animators including Ollie Johnston, Freddie Moore, and Charles Solomon; animator Chuck Jones, best known for creating *Looney Tunes* cartoons; novelist and poet Vladimir Nabokov; Motown founder Quincy Jones; author Truman Capote; playwrights Burt Shevelove,[5] Eugene O'Neill,[6] and Arthur Laurents[7]; composer Nelson Riddle[8]; and writer E.B. White.[9]

Composers Leonard Bernstein and Aaron Copeland regularly used Blackwings, but John Williams used other pencils in addition to Blackwings. I know this because I was part of a 2016 project with Boston Conservatory's president Richard Ortner, who worked at the Boston Symphony Orchestra's Tanglewood with Bernstein and Williams. The Copeland part, Ortner told me, he had researched, and that was why he, too, favored Blackwings—the original versions.

The soft, smooth graphite was a favorite of fashion designer Oscar de la Renta and his wife, Condé Nast magazine editor Françoise de Langlade, the latter of whom would go through boxes of them at a time. "Every top-tier executive has foibles and Francoise is no exception. Every few days she sends out her private secretary to a Madison Avenue stationer to buy Blackwing pencils, No. 2, which cost $3.13 a dozen—and they last only a few days," wrote Marian Christy in the *Boston Globe*.[10] It is worth pointing out that for her column, "Conversations," Christy used old-school skills for an innovative new format. She took notes by hand when others were rushing to use only tape recorders, often asking her subjects "why" questions. When asked in the 1980s by a student reporter about her notetaking, she said that longhand focused her thoughts on what people were saying and on keeping the "good stuff."[11]

Back to Oscar-winning composer John Williams and his pencils. There are photos of him with a variety of pencils, but one brand stands out. In about 1980, Williams sent a used Eagle Electronic Scorer pencil from his desk at the Boston Symphony Orchestra along with a typewritten note to a collector Selwyn Gamble, who had written Williams asking for one of his conductor's batons. Williams, who composed the scores for *Star Wars*, *Schindler's List*, *Jaws*, and *E. T.* hoped it would be a worthy substitution. The pencil and note came up for auction a few years later and sold quickly.[12]

For years it seemed that one of the great pencil mysteries was which brand British novelist Roald Dahl used to write *Charlie and the Chocolate Factory* and *James and the Giant Peach*. The answer can now easily be found at the Roald Dahl

Museum and Story Centre in Missenden, UK, where curators point to the various Dixon Ticonderoga bright yellow pencils. It was an interesting choice for Dahl as that pencil, so common in the United States, was not then exported for sale to the United Kingdom.

(A word about yellow pencils: In the latter part of the nineteenth century, high-quality pencils were not painted. That was the case until Czech pencil makers Koh-i-Noor picked yellow paint as a way to signal that their pencils had sought-after Chinese graphite. In the modern era, yellow pencils became synonymous with US-made pencils, which are also likely to have an attached eraser. During the Second World War, European and UK manufacturers saved on needed supplies by not painting the pencils and not attaching erasers. In the United States, pencil ferrules were made of cardboard or plastic to conserve metal.)

It will come as little surprise that Ernest Hemingway would work in an old-school, deliberate way. Stories about his standing at a table in the morning writing with pencils and pecking away at a manual typewriter have been told of Hemingway, but it is in his posthumously published memoir, *A Moveable Feast*, that we hear from him directly. "The blue-backed notebooks, the two pencils and the pencil sharpener (a pocketknife was too wasteful), the marble-topped tables, the smell of *café crèmes*, the smell of early morning sweeping out and mopping and luck were all you needed," Hemingway wrote.[13]

Yes, novelist John Steinbeck loved and used the Blackwing, but not exclusively. He also liked the Blaisdell's Calculator

600 pencil, the first of which he had stolen from Fox Films, and the Eberhard Faber Mongol, but only the No. 2⅜F, he told the *Paris Review*.[14] They were his go-to until he landed upon the one pencil that he loved above all others.

"I have found a new kind of pencil—the best I have ever had. . . . I think I will always use these. They are called Blackwings and they really glide over the paper," said Steinbeck, the author of *The Grapes of Wrath* and *Cannery Row*. "You know I am really stupid. For years I have looked for the perfect pencil. I have found very good ones but never the perfect one. And all the time it was not the pencils but me. A pencil that is all right some days is not good another day. For example, yesterday, I used a special pencil soft and fine, and it floated over the paper just wonderfully. So, this morning I try the same kind. And they crack on me. Points break and all hell is let loose. This is the day when I am stabbing the paper."[15]

Steinbeck put a lot of thought into his pencils and how long to use each one. A *lot*. "Pencils are a great expense to me and I hope you know it. I buy them four dozen at a time," he told the *Paris Review*. "When in my normal writing position, the metal of the pencil eraser touches my hand, I retire that pencil. Then [my sons] Thom and Catbird get them, and they need pencils. They need lots of pencils. Then I have this kind of pencil and it is too soft. . . . I have fine prejudices, lazy ones and enjoyable ones. It occurs to me that everyone likes or wants to be an eccentric and this is my eccentricity, my pencil trifling. It isn't a very harmful one."[16]

Taking our cue from the master, modern-day pencil fanatics call that stage—when the pencil fits exactly in your writing hand with nothing sticking up—the "Steinbeck Stage." I, however, think that sized pencil should be called the "Edison." Inventor Thomas Edison always carried around a three-inch pencil—about half the size of a regular pencil—that he stored in his vest pocket. If you tour the Edison and Ford Winter Estates in Fort Meyers, Florida, you will find examples of his notebooks filled with sketches and his handwritten notations. "I like my pencil," Edison said. "A fountain pen has always been a mystery to me."[17] So much so that he ordered his custom-made pencils one thousand at a time from the Eagle Pencil Company in grade 5B, which is very soft and leaves broad dark strokes.[18]

The members of the American Constitutional Convention of 1787 used ink and quill to write the founding documents of the United States, but General George Washington carried a pencil around in a Morocco red case.[19] Using a pencil was a habit he picked up while working as a surveyor in what is now Western Pennsylvania and Ohio when he was a young man. Other presidents would favor the pencil, too, for certain tasks.

Abraham Lincoln used a pencil to write the *Gettysburg Address*, including the first draft, which is called the Nicolay copy because the president had given the draft to one of his secretaries John Nicolay. In that version, only the second page is written in pencil, and it shows that the president was still working through some of his ideas in the brilliant speech, which is a mere 272 words.[20] Theodore Roosevelt used pencils for most of his letters, and all of his diaries and drafts of speeches. Herbert Hoover found that using a pencil to write his autobiography kept his writing more disciplined. Franklin Roosevelt doodled with pencils, and Dwight Eisenhower is shown in photographs over the years using pencils.[21]

* * *

Artists seem the most likely to philosophize about their pencil use. Like a great furniture maker, visual artists have reverence for their tools, but know that the craft and the creation is in their use.

> "My pencil is like a fencer's foil." – Andrew Wyeth
> "An animator is an actor with a pencil." – Chuck Jones
> "I have always been a pencil." – Henri de Toulouse-Lautrec
> "Success is a worn-down pencil." – Robert Rauschenberg
> "One must always draw, draw with the eyes, when one cannot draw with a pencil." – Balthus

5 TO BOLDLY GO

To extol the practicality of a pencil is to also admit there are things that a pencil cannot (or should not) do. The best example? A pencil can't be used in space. Well, it *can* write in space, it's just not a great tool to use in the heavens. This reality was firmly set in the Space Race that pitted the United States against the Soviet Union from 1955 to 1975 for every incremental advance in space travel. Pens, even the newer ballpoint pens of the mid-twentieth century, could not write when used upside down much less when there is zero gravity. A pencil would work, but it could break and allow fragments of wood and graphite to float in the craft, and the wood and graphite that make up a pencil are flammable—not a good thing in space.

The inclination to use a pencil by those working on rockets probably extended from the habit of many pilots of keeping a pencil as well as a pen or China Marker handy when marking up maps and charts. Still, astronauts were going to have to make notations, take notes and do calculations while in space, and a writing instrument was something that the National Aeronautics and Space Administration (NASA) had been working on for years. "NASA wanted to avoid pencils because the lead could easily break off and float away, creating a hazard to astronauts and sensitive electronics on the spacecraft," according to a 2021 post on the NASA blog *Spinoff*.[1]

The solution came with the creation of the Space Pen by Paul C. Fisher and his Fisher Pen Company, which had been working on a pressurized pen (one where the ink was pushed to the tip) when word came that NASA needed such a device. "The Fisher Space Pen made its television debut in October 1968, as Apollo 7 mission commander Walter Schirra demonstrated weightlessness by blowing on a pen to control its movement as it floated about the capsule," the *Spinoff* post noted.[2]

This advancement, which would ultimately land Fisher's invention in the permanent collection of the Museum of Modern Art in New York City, should have been heralded for its ingenuity, but instead was turned into a tall tale of US government bloat that centered on how NASA spent millions while the Soviets found a cheaper solution.

The yarn became a standard in Washington, DC, serving as shorthand for government overspending that received a moment in the spotlight in a 2002 episode of the television drama *The West Wing* with two of the show's leading characters, Chief of Staff Leo McGarry (John Spencer) and White House Communications Director Toby Ziegler (Richard Schiff) verbally sparring.

> McGarry: "We spent millions of dollars developing a pen for astronauts that would work in zero gravity. Know what the Russians did?"

Ziegler: "Used a pencil?"

McGarry: "They used a pencil."[3]

Wonderful story. The only problem is, it is not true. Fisher spent millions of his own money to develop the Space Pen, which was widely and quickly adopted into use. "In fact, a pencil is such an impractical alternative in space that cosmonauts also have been using Space Pens since 1969," according to NASA.[4]

You can buy a Fisher Space Pen for less than twenty dollars at REI or Staples, and it's a fun thing to have. Yes, it writes in challenging conditions (upside down, extreme temperatures), but most people don't need a sleek, shiny pen that works in improbable situations. This comes up a lot for those of us with a penchant for stationery products. There's "need" and there's "want" and the latter usually wins. Look, millions of people have tried the powdered drink Tang since NASA sent the orange beverage aboard Friendship 7 for John Glenn on his Mercury flight in 1962. At least the Space Pen looks cool.

Pencils were a favorite among pilots and engineers in the early days of aviation. Yet looking through historical records to learn what specific writing instruments aviators used (did Amelia Earhart or Ted Williams use an Eberhard Faber Mongol?) is like sifting a beach looking for a specific color of sea glass. But a few things can be found including an amazing gem in the Smithsonian Institution's archives. In 2006, when a crew working for the National Air and Space Museum was doing a refurbishment of a US Navy Curtiss

F9C-2 Sparrowhawk fighter biplane, they uncovered a pencil that was, according to the records, "probably lost by a pilot or mechanic in the 1930s."[5]

The artifact is just a stub of a pencil: "Museum personnel found this souvenir from the 1928 Presidential Campaign inside the . . . Sparrowhawk fighter."[6] The blue pencil bears the imprint in white: "Hoover for President 1928." It was an actual campaign collectible from that race in which Republican US Secretary of Commerce Herbert Hoover won forty states to defeat the democratic nominee, New York Governor Al Smith. What you cannot see in the Smithsonian's collection image is that the pencil found in the aircraft is missing a miniature bust of Hoover. There is a similar version (only with a green barrel) for Smith. What makes the findings of the Smithsonian curators more interesting is that the Sparrowhawk was produced in 1932, four years *after* the election. (fig. 4)

Still, the pencil has its place in science and the stars. The Smithsonian Institution's vast collection offers a few things that contradict the idea that pencils played no role in space. One of the items that were transferred with some crew equipment from NASA to the National Air and Space Museum in 2012, when the space shuttle program ended, is a SkilCraft mechanical pencil. "Pens and pencils are among the simplest technologies used in space. Mechanical pencils like this one are preferred to regular pencils because they do not need to be sharpened, thus avoiding bits of wood debris in the crew cabin," according to the museum's item description.

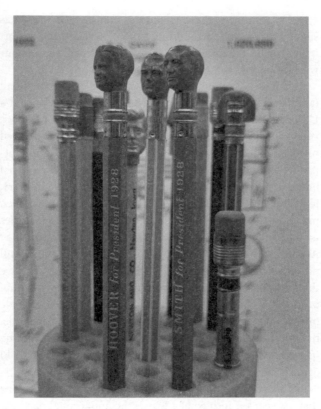

FIGURE 4 A complete "Hoover for President 1928" pencil with other interesting ferrules. Carol Beggy.

"NASA modified these standard commercial products slightly for use in space, adding a piece of Velcro and a short tether cord."[7] The modifications give it a decidedly basement-workshop look.

But let's talk about SkilCraft, a brand that may sound familiar. If you've ever had to write out a mailing label at a US Post Office or complete a form to renew your passport, you've likely used one of the thin, black with silver-colored metal trim, pens that have "SKILCRAFT—U.S. Government" printed in white on the barrel. Since 1968, it's the official brand of pens of the federal government and the US military. SkilCraft pens, and later pencils and notepads, have been made by National Industries for the Blind in five factories in the United States, according to *Opportunity* magazine.[8] According to the SkilCraft website, the consortium still produces between eight and twelve million pens and five thousand other products including office supplies, cleaning products, and uniforms each year. The pen, however, is made to strict standards: it has to write continuously for one mile, the ink should dry in five seconds and not smudge, and the pen must work up to 160 degrees Fahrenheit and down to 40 degrees below zero.[9]

It's usually at this point in the pen/pencil discussions that we veer off into what I fear is the apocryphal part. No matter how much you dig or how hard one presses, there is seemingly no way to check those numbers. There is an oft-repeated list of statistics about the "average pencil" that proves to be similarly tricky when trying to apply some sort of academic rigor to the purported statistics. They are: a seven-inch pencil can produce a line thirty-five miles long, and be sharpened seventeen times. The problem is that when you spot these claims there never appears to be any attribution and thousands of these references show up in searches.

The pencil claim seems to have first been made by the Eagle Pencil Company of New York City, which printed on the back of its yellow office brand pencil, the Mirado: "Scientific durability tests on accurate measuring machines prove that Mirado lead will make a distinct black line well over 35 miles long." It was then part of promotions done by the now-defunct Lead Pencil Manufacturers Association in the late 1950s. (A modern trade group, the Pencil Makers Association, was formed in the early 1970s to certify that the pencils made by member companies were non-toxic and good for use in schools. The PMA, too, promoted the thirty-five-mile claim.)

Because Eagle's advertising copy doesn't solve the riddle, I turned to Andrew Westberg, a knowledgeable pencil collector from the Midwest and president of the American Pencil Collectors Society. When I met him at the APCS's 29th biennial convention in Sioux Center, Iowa, in 2017, among the many things I asked him about was the writing claim. He took a more scientific approach, which he outlined in an email exchange for this book:

The thing about pencils 'facts' is that it depends on so many variables. In theory, a pencil could write a line equal to the circumference of the earth, but that line would be one micron thick. So how much pressure is used while writing becomes really important. . . . I used an Eagle pencil, strapped some paper to a 55-gallon steel drum and started measuring. I tried to get a sense as to how much pressure to put on the tip, I was surprised that the 35-mile number held up. If I were to do it again, I would get a bigger handwriting weight sample and use some high-end measuring tools. . . . I suspect that a slightly heavier hand would greatly reduce the number.

Phew! Now that we know that the length of a pencil's writing ability could be true, what about that sharpener claim? Again, I turned to Westberg. "Seventeen sharpens? Which sharpener, and at what point is it not sharpen-able?" he wrote in the email. "I used an old-fashioned hand crank and stopped when there was no longer enough to hang onto while sharpening. I only did one rotation on the sharpener and got a good point. I think I had more than seventeen 'sharpens' as a result." Most observations are more anecdotal than scientific, but you can "make" a pencil be finished at seventeen spins through the mechanical sharpener, kind of like the Owl and the Tootsie Pop. (As they say on social media: IYKYK.) I have seen people—my Pop-Pop Charlie Beggy, for one—use a pen knife to take away *just* enough wood to keep the pencil sharp enough to write with, keeping it in use for years. Electric sharpeners that love to chew through a pencil to create a point could make the number more like ten "sharpens." I join Westberg in marking this claim as unconfirmed.

Why would I not trust the pencil makers of the mid-twentieth century? I enter into evidence the 1950 ruling by the US Federal Trade Commission (FTC) that Eberhard Faber Co., then of Brooklyn, NY, had falsified claims that its best-selling Mongol pencil stayed "sharper longer than, or are superior in point sharpness to, every other well-known pencil in the same price range," according to an FTC decision filed on June 30, 1950. The stipulation further "calls for the corporation to discontinue claims that scientific laboratory tests of every well-known pencil in the same price range conclusively prove point sharpness superiority for the Mongol pencils by 29 percent."[10] I don't know about "sharpness superiority" but will note that the Mongol was a reliable pencil and I miss the US-made models.

6 COLLECTORS VERSUS USERS

A lot of questions plague pencil people: When does one become a collector? At what point do all these pencils I have become a *collection*? What should I do with all these pencils? Where can I learn more about the types of pencils, the companies that made them, and the people who used them? And, yes, where can I find more?

It was the question of whether anyone else also thought about these things that prompted me to join the American Pencil Collectors Society (APCS), which was founded in Kansas in 1958. As you might expect, it is a decidedly analog organization where your annual dues (ten dollars for US residents) get you a number a member number (I am member number 2228) and copies of the APCS's newsletter, *The Pencil Collector*. It also gives you entrée to a community of people who care about pencils and all things related to collecting them.

Late in 2016, the day's mail brought a copy of the newsletter which had the details of the APCS's biennial national convention, planned for June 2017 in Sioux Center, Iowa, including the note that for more information you should reach out to then–President Ron Brink, the convention's host. I emailed him straight away. He *called* me back within ten minutes. A short time later, I made arrangements to fly out to Sioux Falls, South Dakota, and then drive to Iowa, where the convention was held.

When I arrived at the convention site, I met Brink in person for the first time and he introduced me to the various members setting up for the two-and-a-half-day gathering. I was greeted by each as if we were old friends. I learned a lot from the other members then and still. APCS members tend to pick specialties for collecting: bullet pencils, originally made from spent rifle cartridges; ad tips, which have advertisements on the ferrule; carpenter pencils, most with ads, that are flat and usually brightly colored to make it easier to use them on job sites; brand names, those pencils from manufacturers like Dixon, Blackfeet Indian Writing Company, or Musgrave, usually without ads; and advertising pencils, which are pretty much what you think, but there are sub-categories: those with only full addresses, or from a particular state, or type of business like tractors, sports teams, or hotels. Much of any collection is vintage, with pencils dating back more than one hundred years.

I have met collectors who look for low-numbered (even single-digit) telephone exchanges (from before area codes and seven-digit phone numbers were standard) and at the 2019 convention in Ashland, Ohio, one APCS member had a display of pencils with the phone numbers from one to ninety-nine. Another had pencils that are made to help you dial a rotary phone and phone themed pencils that augment his larger collection of telephone memorabilia. Yet another collector specialized in left-handed pencils. (fig. 5) Yes, left-handed pencils are a thing. It is not like golf clubs or tennis rackets where the equipment is modified to help the left-handed person. These pencils are printed so that type can be read correctly when the pencil is in your left hand. It should be noted that a lefty friend who read a draft of this book pointed out that pencils are kinder than most pens to those who write with their left hand, but pencils can still smudge. That smudge on the page or on the edge of your hand is something that many artists and pencil users have worn as a badge of honor.

If that seems like a lot of pencils, it is. There are APCS members with collections of ten, twenty, and even sixty *thousand* pencils—all sorted, and often cataloged. (In July 2023, APCS Secretary/Treasurer Aaron Bartholmey of Colfax, Iowa, made a bid to set the Guinness World Record for the largest collection with 69,255 pencils counted.[1] He even had a pencil made commemorating the occasion.) Brink, the former APCS president who died in 2019, used to have a ready answer to the question of how big his collection was. He would say something like he had more than 25,000 pencils and six tractors—and he was sure that his wife was thankful it wasn't the other way around.

When asked about collecting pencils by a reporter before that 2017 convention, Brink said: "It's kind of like 'Why

FIGURE 5 What treasures are worth saving and what pencils should be used down to a nub is a personal choice. Carol Beggy.

do people play golf?' It's something that you get interested in, and pretty soon, you can't let it go. It isn't a high-priced hobby."[1] Thankfully, the cost part is true, especially compared to collecting pens, but it can get pricey for some. (In March 2023, a pencil made by Henry David Thoreau's family company sold for two thousand dollars at a charity auction to benefit the Thoreau Society.)[2]

There are some rules about collecting. First, serious collectors want unsharpened pencils but will take a sharpened one for a sought-after or rare find—holding onto it until one in better condition is found. Also, you don't overcharge fellow APCS members or other collectors for finds. And, you should store the pencils in a cool dry place to avoid rot, but there is little you can do to keep erasers fresh.

Finally, you should exercise caution when mailing pencils. Shortly after my membership was announced in the APCS newsletter, I started to receive pencils from members with instructions on how to send things, when, and to whom. I would come to learn that pencils are like first-year college students: there are no circumstances where they should travel alone. It is just not safe out there for a lone pencil. One pencil will break in the mail. Ten will usually arrive unharmed. And while you are packing up, throw in a few stickers or a notebook (a Write notebook for me, please) or something else from the stationery/ephemera world along with a note, usually written in pencil or fountain pen.

I, however, have no discipline when it comes to using or collecting pencils. Zero. None. I would say that I favor brand name pencils, but have acquired a lot of advertising pencils and am sorting the most interesting ones to create a wall display with a map. (Other collectors have sent along pencils to help fill in gaps for that project.) I have many sharpened, vintage, brand name pencils—a lot were given to me by others—and I am thrilled to have them. I could try out the vintage Empire Pencil Lovely, which might rank as my favorite for design and use, Dixon's Cabinet Pencil 720, or a Richard Best Sierra Copying Pencil No. 680 without the guilt of carving up such rare, vintage pencils. (fig. 6)

The pencil is something I collected before I knew that I had a "collection." The first advertising pencils I stashed away were freebies that my dad and grandfather picked up wherever they went. For much of the twentieth century, stores and offices had promotional items out, free for the taking. Dad found pencils at lumber yards, lighting or electronics shops, or at warehouses where he went for supplies. My grandfather would pick them up from politicians, stores, and, I suspect, steal them from any office he went into. Not that Pop Charlie was a thief, just that he liked a good freebie and loved giving things to his grandchildren.

Most collectors have similar stories and most members of the APCS also have pencils with their names and membership number on them, a calling card to be handed out, and something to be traded. There was a point in the latter part of the twentieth century when you could order a dozen pencils, usually from an ad in the back of a magazine, with a name embossed on them. Even those who do not collect pencils can remember the thrill of receiving pencils with their name on them. I got a box of such pencils for my ninth birthday, a gift from my family. I used each one until there was nothing left. I regret all these many years later that I did not save even one. But in acquiring pencils, I have come to own pencils with others' names on them. So, here's to you Frank Species, Quinella Jones, and Meredith Scofield.

To quote The Joker, "So tell me, where does he get all those wonderful toys?" In the pencil world, pencils are often gotten through a variety of places such as stationery stores, eBay for vintage, other collectors for everything, Facebook and other online groups, second-hand shops, estate sales, and auctions.

I once attended an auction in the farm country outside Harrisburg, Pennsylvania, and when it came to a dusty box of mostly sharpened, old pencils, I found myself in a bidding war with some Amish farmers. A friendly person near me talked me out of pushing the bid higher; he had seen it before. Because Amish people do not use mechanized things in their lives, pencils were their go-to communication tool. I immediately stopped bidding on that lot.

Estate and yard sales might not be everyone's idea of fun, but I find them to be an entertaining way to poke around and pick up a few things. After attending a few sales in Southern New England that ranged from posh, high-end to "picker's delight" one spring, I noticed that no matter what house it was, the owners always had the same things, particularly a wooden baseball bat and a pencil sharpener attached to some wall.

"I once had a sale in a super modern home, behind a mechanical gate, and I found a bat behind the master bed," said Maggie Hobbs, co-owner of Hunt Estate Sales in Boston. "In a Chestnut Hill home, safest neighborhood in the US, right? And, get this: the husband used to be on the Bruins, so why not a hockey stick? They had a nook for the kids' homework with a darn pencil sharpener affixed to the wall."

After picking up a large haul of pencils and art supplies once at a Boston area estate sale, I posted some photos of my treasures on Facebook that generated one of the more interesting (legitimate) queries I've ever received on the platform. A person who works in paper restoration and conservation for museums and archives saw my post and asked if they could buy some of the colored pencils and other vintage supplies (paints, inks, and brushes) spotted in the photos. One catch: I could not identify who made the purchase or which institution might be involved. I made a counteroffer: I would send them off for free if the person told me why. Deal. Turns out that conservators and restoration specialists seek out all varieties of items they need to do their jobs of cleaning and repairing books, manuscripts, and works of art. An Eagle Prismacolor Light Green 920 should hold up over time, but better to have several options, and some colors might be discontinued without notice. It is that kind of connection and the interactions with people who I otherwise might not know that has brought me as much joy as actually collecting various pencils. I have that connection, regardless of our backgrounds, home states, religion or political beliefs because of pencils.

* * *

What are the different ferrules called? (Is there *really* a three-knurled ferrule?) Which brands and what individual pencils are the most valuable? (You might not want to ask a question that can't be answered.) How does one learn about pencils? If you're like me, you will always learn new things from others. There is a selected bibliography at the back of this book to give you a start. Doug Martin, who I mentioned in a previous chapter, created his PencilPages.com years ago, and there is Bob Truby's BrandNamePencils.com that keeps up to date on companies and newly discovered pencils. Truby also sells pencils on his site, a one-stop shopping for pencil lovers. Paul Erano publishes the *Fountain Pen Journal*, a print magazine that always has something for pencil lovers.

Like any good reporter, I know who the best sources of information are or where answers can be found. If I have a question about mechanical pencils, I reach out to Jonathan Veley. Colored pencils? Tina or Gary, who I know from online forums. Pencils made in the UK? Dave Tubman's *Pencil Fodder* blog. Japanese- or Canadian-made pencils? There's a guy named John who runs an Etsy shop and is also a good source for information on stickers and so much more. Or, how most pencils write and hold up after a few sharpens? I would turn to Ed in New Jersey, who knows a lot about using pencils and even more about zines. Like any good researcher, I know that there are similar lists of experts and fans for every interest. My list is just that, *my* list, because pencils have not received much historical research beyond Petroski. A friend from college is into model airplanes and rockets, an obsession that started when he was a kid and grew in sophistication as more offerings could be found online that coincided with his professional life providing him with actual disposable income. He rattled off his roster of experts that I tried to follow but got lost somewhere in the discussion of types of fuel and body construction. I'm sure he would nod off when I go down a "type of wood used for pencils" rabbit hole.

Over the years, I've spent hours on websites like WellAppointedDesk.com and BlackwingPages.com, though the latter has been dormant since the 2020 death of its creator, Sean Malone, who was a musician and the foremost authority on the Blackwing 602 as his avocation. I miss communicating with Malone about pencils. He was the first person I would reach out to when I found some new (to me) reference to a Blackwing or Van Dyke pencil, and after his death, I had to stop myself from emailing him when I met someone whose father had worked for Eberhard Faber in Mountain Top, Pennsylvania.

Discussions and even debates on Reddit and in Facebook groups are great places to learn new things. For example: an eraser from a jumbo pencil sold at Home Depot will fit a vintage bullet pencil, and "pencils up" means to stop writing, but "pencils down" means to stop writing and let go of the pencil. Not scientific, but interesting. I truly miss the early days of Tumblr, before things got out of hand there, when you might see a posting by an artist of their work and the tools they used to create the piece.

I know that there are some out confused by the thought that there are members of a pencil collecting group who travel great distances to meet with their fellow collectors. A quick Internet search nets scores of such hobby groups. Those include the National Valentine Collectors Association; the National International Harvester Collectors Club, and the National Fishing Lure Collectors Club.

If meetups IRL (in real life, of course) are more your thing, there's the National Association of Milk Bottle Collectors, which held its convention in Sturbridge, Massachusetts, in May 2023. The Antique Barbed Wire Society had five events on its 2023 calendar, and, The Ice Screamers, a group that seeks "to preserve ice cream history" organized its July 2023 convention in York, Pennsylvania, to share space with the Antique Advertising Association of America's gathering.[3] To sum it up, collectors are everywhere, collecting just about everything.

It all begs the question, who collects? Like anyone with a favorite product, pencil users face the reality of business and marketing just like those who collect sneakers, comic books, or notebooks. There is always someone making a limited edition or special edition "collectible," and then there is the vintage market. There are role-playing gamers (some famous like Vin Diesel and Joe Manganiello) who favor certain pencils and very specific notebooks, chosen for both the quality and the layout for playing *Dungeons & Dragons*. There is a woman in Wisconsin who turned her collection into the World Museum of Writing Instruments, a guy in Ohio that ran a museum of pencil sharpeners, and yet another fan currently starting a museum to the pencil grinders in Texas. Some users keep just the last bit of the pencils that they have worn down—they are called stubs, nubbins, or nubs—and hold onto them in jars or on displays.

The rest usually enter through a love of writing, creating art, or their profession. In the pencil world, we refer to pencils as a "gateway drug" because soon you'll be buying up notebooks, sharpeners, erasers, pens, and antique blotters. We have a category name for all of that other stuff, too: pencil adjacent. There's also an acronym for a collection— some might say hoard or mess—that has grown very (very) large: SABLE, which stands for Stash Acquisition Beyond Life Expectancy.

* * *

If I had a bigger house, I'd have more pencils, books, typewriters, and other such things. Anyone's collection should bring them joy from the thrill of the hunt or the satisfaction of acquisitions. But, too often, there is the problem of what to do with a collection after you die. Ron

Brink's family reached out to his friends at APCS and I was both saddened and honored to acquire some of his pencils at that first convention after his death.

Don't worry about me, however. My sister has a plan. When I die, she wants to hold an old-fashioned Irish-American wake for me at my house. You'll enter the front door, pass through the living room (my house doesn't have a parlor, alas), pay your respects, and on your way out, you can take a book and some pencils (stuff them in a tote bag that I picked up at some book convention) before exiting the house out the back door (the one with the wooden baseball bat) to an open bar on the patio.

It will be a fun party; too bad I won't be around for it.

7 PENCILS IN THE WILD

There's a saying that when you are a hammer, everything's a nail. The correlating theory is that once you notice them, you see pencils everywhere.

Take for example the opening ceremonies for Super Bowl LIII, the National Football League's championship game in which the New England Patriots faced off against the Los Angeles Rams on February 3, 2019, in the Mercedes-Benz Stadium in Atlanta, Georgia. The first thing the superstitious fans of the Patriots spotted was that head coach Bill Belichick was wearing one of his signature sweatshirts with the cut-off sleeves in blue, which had proved lucky in the past—not in red as he had in Super Bowl XLII in 2008, when the Patriots lost.[1]

When the camera cut to Belichick with a Blackwing behind his right ear instead of the usual yellow Dixon Ticonderoga, the excitement really began for eagle-eyed pencil spotters. There also was a bit of concern that the switch to Blackwing might cause a turn of bad luck. That worry was thankfully short-lived as the Patriots beat the Rams in a 13-to-3 win. Pencil tucked firmly behind the coach's ear for all the world to see.

Pencil sightings are ubiquitous in television shows, particularly those with newsrooms, law offices, or police stations, with one standing out above the rest: *M*A*S*H*. Set in a mobile hospital unit in the Korean War, the show, which ran from 1972 to 1983, never hit a wrong note when it came to the pencils, typewriters, and pens the characters used. All were correct to the time period, at least according to the fans who fill up the various online discussion forums.

Tune into practically any episode of the show and you'll see Radar using a stub of a pencil and a beat-up metal clipboard for the day's duty roster. Or Hawkeye jotting down some orders on a medical chart with an eraser-less pencil that is brown or unpainted instead of a bright yellow. Or head nurse Margaret Houlihan using a pencil and then tucking it away behind her right ear. That authenticity came from so many US military veterans working on the show and so many longtime writers who had used the same tools themselves working during the 1950s. The deepest diving fans will note that the show's star, the award-winning actor, writer, and director Alan Alda, served in the Army, including a stint in South Korea after the fighting had ended.[2] In a wonderful 2023 confluence of technology, Alda asked OpenAI's artificial intelligence chatbot ChatGPT to write a new scene for *M*A*S*H*. The result, which Alda covered on his podcast *Clear+Vivid*, is, well, just not funny. It features

Alda's Hawkeye and B.J. Hunnicutt, played by the definitely funny Mike Farrell, having a back-and-forth about Hawkeye's underwear.[3]

The interesting twist for me is that technology such as artificial intelligence has made pencil spotting (and pencil collecting, and sleuthing pencil history and trivia) easier. Whether looking for pencils, reviewing the titles of books on the shelves in scenes (it's a thing, just search social media), or indulging other obsessions, technological advances from streaming services to online databases to algorithms on social media to YouTube videos have made it easier to find more of the things that interest you. That and the fact that you can get a 75-inch television from your nearest big box store to view what you find.

Some television series, like *Perry Mason* and *Gunsmoke*, had the advantage of being filmed while the US pencil industry was in its prime. Other shows that stand out are *The Wire*, *Law & Order* (the original series), *Gilmore Girls*, and *Mad Men*. Numerous scenes that are regularly referenced include one from the first episode of *Dharma & Greg*, where Greg is seen throwing pencils up toward the ceiling to see if he could make the pointy ends stick in the tiles in the suspended ceiling. I mentioned this once to a friend and he immediately recited several more shows that had a similar scene or ongoing joke: *How I Met Your Mother*, *The X-Files*, *Castle*, and *Coach*. There was a running bit for many years on *Late Night with David Letterman* in which the host would throw some of his pencils and many of the cards he wrote on through fake windows to the sound effect of glass breaking. Seth Meyers, now host of *Late Night*, has had pencils on his desk since his first show and has said that the football team pencils remind him of his days in elementary school in Michigan.[4] And, the original late night pencil lover was Johnny Carson, who would spin his pencils with erasers on both ends while talking to his guests.

The pencils do not have to be of high quality or used by renowned artists to elicit a response from the pencil people. There was a storyline on the police drama *Major Crimes*, which ran in the latter part of the 2010s, with a person writing letters to intimidate a witness using fictional "Red Wings" pencils. That a serial rapist and killer would use a particular brand of pencils and special notebooks did not squelch the discussion about the type of pencil and paper that was used.

But that is dwarfed by a movie hero, although a very violent one, who is the champion of pencil spotters everywhere: John Wick, the retired hitman who is forced out of retirement to seek vengeance on the mobsters who killed his puppy, the last gift from his late wife. Played with a cool and dampened demeanor by Keanu Reeves, Wick is said to be so good at his job that he did the impossible. The scene of Wick's exploits has spawned thousands (tens of thousands?) of GIFs and memes and goes like this: The head of the Russian mob, Viggo Tarasov (Michael Nyquist), tries to explain to his son, Iosef (Alfie Allen), why angering Wick wasn't his best course of action.

Viggo: Well, John wasn't exactly the Boogeyman. He was the one you sent to kill the [expletive] Boogeyman.

Iosef: Oh . . .

Viggo: John is a man of focus, commitment, sheer will—something you know very little about. I once saw him kill three men in a bar—with a pencil, with a [expletive] pencil.[5]

That scene from the first Wick movie in 2014 echoes through the franchise and is given an epic reprise in 2023's *John Wick: Chapter 4*, according to the reviews in my family. It is not, however, for the gentle folk who want to collect pencils and not use them as weapons.

The pencil was also used as a weapon in 2022 on the Korean television show *The Glory*, and we know exactly which pencil: Staedtler's Mars Lumograph, with its distinctive blue and black design. The German company's pencil went viral after one of the show's actors, Song Hye Kyo, takes a Lumograph out of her hair and uses it on some bullies for a very John Wick result. The Lumograph later sold out and is now a fashion accessory a la Song's bun with a blue and black pencil in it.[6]

On a more nostalgic front, there is the 2022 film *Tár*, starring Cate Blanchett which chronicles the downfall of fictional composer and conductor Lydia Tár. Yeah, yeah, many awards, six Oscar nominations—but did you catch the scene when the conductor opens up a cupboard to reveal a stash of vintage, Eberhard Faber Blackwing 602s? For those of us who love our writing and drawing devices, this moment was as dramatic as when Dorothy walked into the Technicolor world of Oz. Tár's shelves are packed with the kind of finds that one (of "us," at least) hopes are out there still. The folks at the sleek and crisp stationery store Present & Correct in London calculated the cost of that cabinet and posted on social media to great response. Using both eBay and recommended retail prices, they determined that the eight boxes of newly made Blackwing Era pencils would run two hundred and eighty British pounds. The five boxes of the original Eberhard Faber Blackwing 602s would fetch two thousand and thirty-one pounds, and the twelve boxes of modern Blackwings can be had for nine thousand two hundred and sixty-four. That's a total of £11,575 eleven thousand five hundred and seventy-five pounds, or thirteen thousand nine hundred and thirty-one US dollars, as calculated at the time of the 2022 posting on the platform that was then called Twitter.

The conductor favoring Blackwing is an authentic representation of the many musicians who used the Blackwing 602, as mentioned earlier, because the flattened ferrule keeps the pencil from rolling off a music stand. Similarly, the 602's siblings, the Van Dyke 601 and the Microtomic 603 (both were made by Eberhard Faber and had flat ferrules with adjustable erasers), were the go-to for architects and engineers because they stayed put and came in various lead grade cores.

That the character Lydia Tár has a stash of the coveted pencil is also a product of the film's writer-director Todd Field, who trained as a musician and uses the original

Blackwing. "For instance, he writes his scripts longhand with vintage, discontinued Blackwing pencils, sharpened only with a KUM Masterpiece sharpener," according to a profile of Field in *W Magazine*.[7]

That pencils are worthy of such serious ardor has prompted some serious scrutiny in articles, journals, blogs, and on podcasts, but perhaps the pencil's greatest recognition came in the form of a college class: The University of Oregon course called "HC 101H: The Pencil," created and taught by Daniel Rosenberg, a professor in the Department of History. It was a full four credit-course that met twice a week. The course description caught my eye: "If you pay attention to such things, you'll have noticed that the pencil has been having a comeback. In 2010, the iconic Blackwing 602 Pencil, manufactured by the Eberhard Faber Pencil Company from the 1930s, was reintroduced. After its discontinuation in the 1990s, aficionados had been hoarding dead stock, and the resale market had gone crazy."[8] (I feel so seen!) Rosenberg goes on to list other analog topics and related history before ending the description with a reading list and a homework assignment. "Students are asked to obtain a pencil before the first class session."[9] Oh, have I got a stash for you, students.

I hardly finished reading the course info when I fired off an email to the professor (one instance when technology has its advantages). I was curious about what prompted him to offer such a class.

"I was not a pencil aficionado prior to designing the course. I've always liked pencils, but never really thought about them a lot. The course came about because of COVID," Rosenberg wrote in an email. He continued,

> In spring term 2020, like most everyone, I was suddenly teaching online. It was a strange experience. By chance, the course I was teaching that term was a course on the history of the Internet. That turned out to be a godsend. All of a sudden, my students and I were newly reliant on Internet technology for pretty much everything, and all of us wanted to know what it was all about. The course turned out to be the best I had ever taught. Everyone was *so* engaged and present (if you will).

The course was his effort to build on that. "Then summer came, and I was designing a new course for incoming [students]. But these [first-year students] wouldn't be coming to campus, or if they were coming to campus, they wouldn't be coming to the classroom," Rosenberg wrote.

> My challenge was to think of a way to give them an experience of each other and an experience of Eugene, that was "present" in a real and interesting way. I knew from my experience the previous spring that I could teach a great course about "distance" over the Internet. I was curious whether I could teach a great course about "presence."

His historian training took over, Rosenberg said, and as he was thinking about Oregon history (for the sense of place),

FIGURE 6 Thoreau is represented on the New York Public Library's Literary Walk with a quote from a 1969 play. Eileen McGill.

his research of the history of the timber industry, led to wood products, which led him to pencils. Not surprisingly his reading list includes *Walden*.

How much we all recognize the resurgence of pencils or any analog item is particularly interesting in the context of its connections to the past. Innumerable people have passed by Claes Oldenburg and Coosje van Bruggen's large-scale sculpture *Typewriter Eraser, Scale X*, a Brobdingnagian depiction of, you guessed it, a typewriter eraser with a spinning wheel and brush in the National Gallery of Art Sculpture Garden in Washington, DC. But how many actually know how that typewriter eraser worked? Do they need to know its purpose to appreciate its beauty? No, they don't.

I love when public art is mixed with my private obsessions. One of my favorites is the New York Public Library's Library Walk, a celebration of notable literary figures with quotes and art that runs along East 41st Street, starting at Park Avenue. Thoreau, who is represented in the library's collection, including a Thoreau family-made pencil, appears twice along the walk. One is his quote about books, "Books are the treasured wealth of the world . . ." and the other is from Robert E. Lee and Jerome Lawrence's 1969 play, *The Night Thoreau Spent in Jail*. The plaque offers the Thoreau character's quote: "Writing your name can lead to writing sentences. And the next thing you'll be doing is writing paragraphs, and then books. And then you'll be in as much trouble as I am!" (Fig. 6)

8 A THOREAU JOB

It was an August day and the sun was almost too bright for the tourists in Concord, Massachusetts, wandering by the shops and sights along Main Street in the town's center. A quarter of a mile away at the Sleepy Hollow Cemetery, the towering mature trees provided enough shade to give a welcome break from the heat.

Tucked into a back corner of the historic cemetery are the graves of some of the best-known US writers and thinkers in the mid- to late-nineteenth century along Authors Ridge. You will find naturalist, surveyor, and writer Henry David Thoreau with his family, not far from the Alcotts—nearly all of them—essayist and philosopher Ralph Waldo Emerson, and novelist Nathaniel Hawthorne. The section is up on a crest and not an easy walk, but streams of people follow the signs with crooked arrows that read: "To / Authors Ridge / Graves of / Thoreau / Hawthorne / Alcotts / Emerson." Even by cemetery standards, the visitors on the day that I stopped by seemed to approach the grave sites with an extra quiet reverence.

The region serves as a memorial to the earliest days of the United States and the cultural explosion of the 1840s through the post-Civil War 1870s. It was here that Thoreau, who among his many jobs was a pencil maker, and Emerson would walk so often that a modern "Emerson-Thoreau Amble" is marked out and connects the town of today to Walden Pond. In the eighteenth century, this path and others that have now been rebuilt as highways, homes, and retail outlets still showed the scars of the Revolutionary War that ended just twenty years before Emerson's birth.

Henry David Thoreau (1817-1862) was a well-known figure in his day, and his life and death still garner attention. Back at Sleepy Hollow Cemetery, the Thoreau family area is marked by an imposing granite marker with each family member's details carved onto it. Off to the side, you'll find Henry's modest headstone that measures about two-unsharpened-pencils across and the same height at the center peak and has only one word, "Henry." (fig. 7) If there is a protagonist of the American pencil story, it is Thoreau. When writing his book on the pencil, Petroski devotes the opening of his first chapter to Thoreau and how he made lists of everything he used each day, what was in his cabin in the woods, and the animals, trees and weather he spotted along the way. Everything except for the pencil he used to write the lists or catalog the wildlife seen.[1]

Maybe Thoreau saw the pencil as a given since his family owned a pencil-making factory that a young Henry modernized. The pencils made at Thoreau & Company

FIGURE 7 Henry David Thoreau's grave in his family plot at the Sleepy Hollow Cemetery in Concord, Massachusetts. Carol Beggy.

(sometimes John Thoreau listed "and sons") were considered to be superior because of the graphite they used.[2] Henry's writing is missing references not to just pencils but to other tools that he used. Unlike those curious researchers who came before us who had to pore over hundreds of pages, we can just find an electronic copy of *Walden; or, Life in the Woods* online and search for "pencils." I did it for you, and there are two "pencil" references in the piece.[3]

Not surprisingly, Henry's grave is often covered with pencils, bird nests, pinecones, and other things that evoke his life's work. In 2017, a survey marker was placed at the Thoreau family plot to mark Henry David Thoreau's "Final Point," as measured by the Surveyors Historical Society. Buried nearby is Henry's younger sister, Sophia, who should be noted for her success in getting Henry's work published posthumously and for her efforts as a naturalist and observer.[4]

(Let's get something out of the way; just how is Thoreau pronounced? Some say "THOR-oh," but it seems that those in Concord favor "THUR-oh." At the Walden Pond Gift Shop and the Concord Museum, the staff appeared to use the latter, but what better evidence is there than local puns? There's "Thoreauly Antiques" on Walden Street, and a curb-side message board near the Concord Public Library in the summer of 2022 that said, "*Walden* is a classic due to Thoreau editing.")

Back to our amble: Just a bit further up the cemetery path on the Ridge, you'll find Ralph Waldo Emerson (1803-1882) and Nathaniel Hawthorne (1804-1864). Emerson's headstone is between the graves of both of his wives, in a section gated off and decidedly more elaborate than that of the Thoreau family. In his 1836 book-length essay *Nature*, Emerson outlined the basic tenets of Transcendentalism, a philosophical movement that holds that there is inherent goodness in people and nature and that people are at their best when they are self-reliant and independent of institutions.[5] I am not sure if it by is sheer will or brute strength that some people manage to get pencils to Emerson's stone as a tribute to the writer.

Like Thoreau, Hawthorne worked as a surveyor and found a full life in Concord, where he raised his family. His novels include *The Scarlet Letter* and *The House of Seven Gables*, which is an actual house turned museum in Salem, Massachusetts. On the day of my walk, his grave was also covered in pencils, plastic pens, and a copy of one of his novels.

The first thing I noticed while approaching Louisa May Alcott's grave was the US Army veteran medallion and an American flag near her headstone. Had I not been tipped off by a historian friend, I might have thought they were in recognition of one of her many male family members and or other veterans nearby.. Alcott (1832-1888) received the honor for her service during the Civil War at the Union Hotel Hospital near Washington, DC, according to the historical markers. Even though it is flush with the ground, her headstone is easily spotted with the dozens of pencils and other tributes to her writing piled around it. Among Alcott's teachers was Thoreau—see how it all comes around?—who inspired her to write the poem *Thoreau's Flute* about her time at Walden Pond, which was published in *The Atlantic* in 1863.[6]

All the Alcotts are buried near Louisa, except May, Louisa's youngest sister. Louisa based her *Little Women* character Amy on May. (The fanatics in online forums and social media love to point out that Amy is an anagram of May, although not a particularly tough one to decipher.) May Alcott Nieriker (1840-1870) was buried in Paris where she had lived for several years. You'd be forgiven if you thought that May, an artist who established a solid reputation for her skill, was buried with the other Alcotts as Louisa had a headstone for her sister placed at the family plot in Sleepy Hollow. I spied more than a few pencils and paintbrushes left at May's memorial, too.

Not far from Authors Ridge is the grave of Daniel Chester French, the sculptor of the seated Abraham Lincoln at the Lincoln Memorial and the John Harvard statue in the Yard at Harvard University. French's connection to Concord dates to his teen years when his family moved there after the Civil War. Shortly after their arrival, May Alcott, who trained at the School of the Museum of Fine Arts in Boston, started French (1850-1931) on his path as an artist when she gave him modeling clay and tools, and some instruction on how to use them.[7]

French's first notable commission was the Concord Minute Man statue located in the national park for which it is named, near the site where, in 1775, the first colonial militia were killed, marking the start of the Revolutionary War. The seven-foot statue sits on a stone base that has the opening quatrain of Emerson's poem "Concord Hymn"—with the famous "the shot heard round the world" line—carved into it.[8] French would ultimately move to Stockbridge in Western Massachusetts, where he built a studio, complete with railroad tracks so that he could take his massive creations outside to be viewed in natural light. Walking through his studio and around the wooded acreage nearby, you get a sense that French was trying to recreate the Concord of his youth, or at least maintain that feeling of living surrounded by nature with a connection to the world at large.

The Concord of a generation before the Civil War and the towns just west of it were where American pencil-making began. Thoreau rightly gets all the credit for his innovations and the quality of the graphite produced at the family facility, but William Munroe (1778-1861) was the first person to properly manufacture pencils in the United States. It should be noted that the historians at the Concord Museum credit an anonymous "girl who, while at school in Medford, Massachusetts, made pencils from graphite recycled from used pencil ends" as the *first* Concord pencil maker.[9] That detail perfectly encapsulates why I love historians.

Munroe, a cabinetmaker, was looking for more work for his shop in 1812 and, ultimately settled on pencils.[10] The area was perfect for such work. There were a lot of trees, mills powered by rivers, and natural supplies of graphite.

Petroski says that it took Munroe ten years to think he was producing high-quality pencils.[11] Much of his work was lost to time and history as Munroe's pencils were not imprinted with the maker's name (something that the Thoreaus did). While a Thoreau pencil is more easily spotted, those made by the Thoreaus, Munroe, and Benjamin Ball are all easily recognizable by looking at the core. From the 1820s into the 1840s pencils were made with a square core in round, wood-case pencils. Modern pencils have round cores. (fig. 8)

It was the appropriately named Ebenezer Wood (1792-1880) and his pencil-making operation just west of Concord in Acton, Massachusetts, who first used a circular saw and created octagonal- and hexagonal-shaped pencil barrels.[12] Most pencils manufactured in the later-nineteenth and twentieth centuries were made with round cores and had either a hexagonal or round case. Although Wood would work in several of the factories, the site of his shop is marked today as the "Nashoba Brook Pencil Factory Site" in a conservation area far off the tourist maps.

Munroe is buried in the family plot at Sleepy Hollow Cemetery. (No pencils were left to mark his contributions when I approached the area , but maybe one or two were left after.)

John Thoreau and his sons got into the pencil business by way of graphite and plumbago. After producing pencils for a while, the company shifted to just selling graphite for pencils and refining it for typographers who used it in electrotyping, a printing method that accurately duplicated

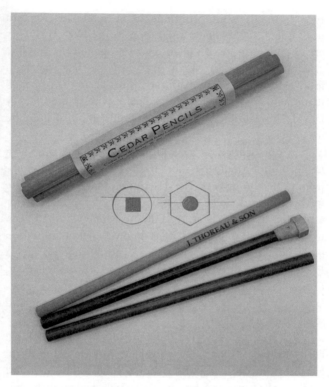

FIGURE 8 The cores of pencils produced in the 19th century were made square with a round, wood casing surrounding it, as shown in this drawing. In the last century, almost all pencils have cores that are round with a hexagonal-shaped wood case. Also shown are pencils with square graphite cores and a reproduction of a John Thoreau & Son pencil that is sold at the Walden Pond gift shop in Concord, Mass. Carol Beggy.

type.[13] Pencils would continue to be made in Concord until about 1875 when a migration to the New York City area began with Joseph Dixon, who reopened his graphite crucible company in Northern New Jersey. He was soon followed by other manufacturers. Most accounts of pencil manufacturing state that it was Dixon who trained Henry David Thoreau and others in the preparation of graphite for pencils.

It is no surprise, to me at least, that Henry's time as a manufacturer would be short-lived. He tended to bounce from project to project. The description that Thoreau wrote for his Harvard College Class of 1837 notes, published for a reunion ten years later, read like someone who had been working twice as long: "I don't know whether mine is a profession, or a trade, or what not. . . . I am a Schoolmaster—a Private Tutor, a Surveyor—a Gardener, a Farmer—a Painter, I mean a House Painter, a Carpenter, a Mason, a Day-Laborer, a Pencil-Maker, a Glass-paper Maker, a Writer, and sometimes, a Poetaster."[14]

What interests me is what Thoreau lists and what he doesn't. He listed "writer," but much of his paid work was journalism. He has been called a philosopher because of *Walden* and *Civil Disobedience* and his study of Transcendentalism, but others, particularly in the twentieth century did not give him much credit as a philosopher. I have always been interested in Thoreau as a poet, something he claimed in his time, but the community hasn't always claimed him. Thoreau, it seems, falls in and out of favor with the poetry crowd, but was a strong influence on Robert Frost, who, it turns out, now falls in and out with the poetry gatekeepers.

On the centennial of Thoreau's death, Frost, then eighty-eight years old, participated in a commemoration and stated that *Walden* is "One of the greatest books we have had in America—and it will always be."[15] Frost credited Thoreau with inspiring him to use the natural world as a catalyst. "When I am weary of my considerations and I cannot stand it any longer, I always say: 'Me for the woods!'"[16]

Whether *Walden* was philosophy or poetry wasn't something that Frost wrestled with—it was poetry to him. This is something that I discussed with Zachary Bond, a bookseller, poet, and teacher. After much discussion, we concluded: Thoreau's writing is lyrical and poetic. The rest is a question of whether or not it resonates with the reader more than 150 years after his death. Bond wrote out his further thoughts and shared them with me.

To write a poem is to explore an unknown space and to embrace not knowing where one might end up. The greatest poems use old words to find new ways of talking about the world. This sort of intentional aimlessness, this search less for answers than their questions, is central to the whole project of *Walden*. Like great poets, Thoreau is content to live amidst his many contradictions or, as [John] Keats put it "capable of being in uncertainties, mysteries, doubts, without any irritable reaching after fact and reason."

Thoreau's poems were written out of his passing thoughts, which were, like so much of his writing, captured in notebooks and diaries. There is an oft-repeated statement that Henry was never without a pencil to record all of his thoughts and observations, and thanks to the visitors of Sleepy Hollow Cemetery, he never is.

9 PENCILS UP

It's been decades since I sat in a classroom on a Saturday morning to take the SAT test, but I still remember my frayed nerves and anxious stomach as the proctor read through the many rules and regulations that would guide our day. The tests, which until recently carried a lot of weight in admission to certain elite colleges, were day-long affairs with short breaks between sections on math and verbal skills. I cannot recall one question asked, but I do remember finding comfort in the only things you could take with you to your test: two No. 2 pencils and an eraser. It won't surprise anyone who knows me (or perhaps those of you who have read this far) that I carried extras of both in my bookbag. No need for a sharpener, all classrooms had hand-crank models mounted to the walls.

Not only do I remember the pencils, I know which ones I used: promotional ad pencils from Parkway Electric, the electrical contracting company that my dad started in 1973. This isn't a guess that I would probably take a pencil from the family operation. I am certain of my choice of No. 2s because Dad let me order this round of promo items—and there was a screwup in the order. This was a time before online submissions or even Fax machines; you sent the order and your items were shipped in return.

When the ten grosses of pencils arrived at the office with a thud, I ran out to open the box and my joy immediately turned to horror when I looked at the printing: "No Job To Small." I came into the office and showed my dad, who calmly asked me if I thought I had made the mistake. No, I assured him, adding that Mom had typed it up and would have kept a copy. He didn't say another word to me and dialed up the company. After a lively go-round, another batch arrived a week or so later with the correct saying: "No Job Too Small."

We asked if the company wanted the misprinted versions returned and the salesman told us to keep them, so we donated them to the area schools. My dad joked that he got more business from the "wrong" pencils than from other items we ordered over the years. I can still see the classroom on that morning of the SAT, most of my classmates sitting at desks with two No. 2 Parkway Electric pencils with the homophone mishap. I hope those pencils brought them as much luck as they did me.

While the SAT and other tests for high school placement and college and graduate school entrance were still using pencils as this book was being written, the College Board announced that by 2024 it will be pencils down forever when the SAT test process is completely computerized. It was also announced the test itself will be cut to about two hours, the reading passages will be shortened, and they are working on making the questions fairer to all test takers, according to the *New York Times*.[1] For this reader, the most interesting part of the media coverage that day was that students find computerized less stressful than using a pencil or pen to mark scoring sheets. Clearly a generational divide has been drawn.

An unscientific scan at the beginning of 2023 of a bay of test preparation books at the Coop, Harvard University's bookstore, found nearly thirty different book covers with an image of a pencil or an eraser or the point of the pencil filling in an answer on a scoring sheet. It isn't just limited to the test prep section of bookstores because pencils function as symbols for education in other ways, too.

Take for example Tara Westover's 2018 memoir *Educated*, about growing up in and leaving her survivalist family to attend a few of the best universities in the world. The cover shows a small, silhouetted figure atop "a mountain" that is actually the tip of a sharpened pencil. Psychologist and Nobel laureate Daniel Kahneman's 2011 book on judgment and decision-making, *Thinking, Fast and Slow*, has a well-worn pencil, with loads of teeth marks. Book buyers and even casual browsers will get the gist of the book at first sight. Pencil fans will also notice that the art department chose a Mongol pencil, with its unmistakable gold stripe on the ferrule. Kahneman's 2021 book, *Noise: A Flaw in Human Judgment*, which he wrote with Olivier Sibony and Cass R. Sunstein, also uses the worn and chewed Mongol pencil motif of the earlier release. And, among dozens of others, the best-selling novel *Lessons in Chemistry* by Bonnie Garmus features an illustrated image of a woman with glasses and a yellow pencil in the bun in her hair with the words "a novel" where the No. 2 writing would normally be.

There's a word for this. Skeuomorph. The actual definition of which is: "an ornament or design representing a utensil or implement."[2] It goes beyond the imagery, the iconography, or iconology. It is when the pencil itself is shorthand for what a pencil can do.

That pencil as a symbol was what prompted me to check in with Tim and Nicole Delger of the marketing and design firm Studio Delger of Nashville, Tennessee. I have admired their work with Musgrave Pencil Company, which included not just helping to spread the word about this legacy brand, but in giving the pencil packaging and boxes a boost. They also worked on new offerings such as that Single Barrel 106 (the one I swooned over in the second chapter), and a late 2022 release: the round-barrel, purple-painted Pencil King, which came about from the Delgers's work with Musgrave to use some old dies and stamps that were found in the Musgrave plant in Middle Tennessee.

That imagery of a pencil on a cover of a test prep book is obvious, but it conveys something deeper, too. "I think pencils convey limitless potential, where ideas come from," said Nicole. "A pencil is about learning, about taking action, about creating."

Since they worked with the graphic imagery *and* actual pencils, I wanted to know if they thought it was odd that an object that is seemingly used less and less appeared to be used more and more to signify "write here" or "you need to fill in the information here" even in electronic communication. "When you are scheduling something, you see a pencil. When you need to change something, there is a pencil icon," Tim told me on a Zoom call. "I think of the phone image. I think there are people who have never touched an old-fashioned telephone handset, but they know what to do."

That telephone icon is easily recognized and is used in airports, hospitals, and government offices around the world. The pencil also sparks an immediate connection. "It's not like a kid in kindergarten has ever used an actual telephone, but they have used a pencil. So, I think people make the connection with a pencil quickly," Tim said.

Words can evoke an image, too. A headline on a *New York Times* story in October 2022 said: "When a Sharpened Pencil Just Isn't Enough."[3] I was impressed by the headline writer's skill (it is a specific job and not easily done well) in conveying that there is more to supporting education efforts than providing supplies. The two words—"sharpened pencil"—pull the reader right in.

Using pencils has always been a part of Tim's artistic expression; even in an era of iPads and electronics, his creative efforts start with pencils. "Everything I do starts with a sketch," Tim said, noting that before they started working with Musgrave, he had containers full of pencils in his work spaces. Now, there are boxes and cases and stacks around him of pencils in various stages of sharpening that were used in photography for social media and other marketing. Yes, they said, their office smells like cedar. "I always go back to pencil," Tim said. "It focuses your attention and then you can get to work."

The use of a pencil at the start of creativity also holds for Boston artist and author Bren Bataclan. Some years ago, I learned about Bataclan's art through an ongoing project where he or a friend would leave paintings around the city for people to find. The project has since been expanded internationally. One day in January 2012, as I was leaving a doctor's appointment in Massachusetts General Hospital's Yawkey Building, I stopped in a sitting area in the upstairs lobby and found one of his paintings. It's an 8- by 12-inch picture of a smiling baseball on a bright green background that came with a note that says: "This painting is yours if you promise to smile at random people more often." I scooped it up and it now hangs where I can see it as I am getting ready for my day.

About ten years later, Bataclan created a mural at the Morse Elementary School in Cambridge, Massachusetts, at the request of art teacher Ami Kerr, and even before he signed it, I knew who the artist was. Bataclan's distinctive style is clearly influenced by anime; the bright-colored images with dark borders were clues, but the dead giveaway was the pencil strokes left on the wall, just as they are on my painting of a baseball. I asked Bataclan about it and he told me that it is not only intentional but necessary. "I don't erase my pencil lines for the following reasons: When students draw with me, I ask them not to erase. I tell them that everything they create with me is going to be beautiful and perfect," he wrote in an email. "With that in mind, I follow my own rules. I also think that it's OK to show mistakes and the process."

That act of pure creation is something I was allowed to experience as a child at my family's "camp," a cottage compound where several families have been spending summer weekends for more than 115 years. One of the dads was a man named Stuart Harris, a banker by trade and a painter at heart. Mr. Harris—the kids would not have called him Stu—would beautifully adorn anything that wasn't (or was) nailed down. He would grab a pencil, lightly sketch out what he was going to paint, and start mixing the colors on his palette.

One day, while he was working on a short bench that was barely big enough to fit two adults, Mr. Harris pointed to a circle drawn in pencil and handed me the paintbrush that he had just loaded with a bright yellow. I painted a bit and after I finished, he sent me on my way. When I came back later there were two beautiful flowers painted on the bench with "What a pair of daisies!" written below. For years, I would walk by the bench and think of how a man with some vision, a pencil, and a brush, had encouraged a child to believe that she could create anything.

10 #FINDYOURPEOPLE

It usually starts simply, often in a post on social media, with someone saying, "I'm new to pencil collecting and I am wondering about [a pencil brand or pencil-adjacent item]." That opening is, in my experience, met quickly with solid, thought-out answers, links for more information on how the desired item could be acquired, offers from more experienced pencil people to send along pencils, erasers, notebooks or sharpeners (always with a handwritten note and a few stickers thrown in), or a gentle nudge toward the search function to look for previous posts. But that opening query is always met with a hearty round of welcomes and various forms of #FindYourPeople comments. Like many subcultures, the pencil-pen-stationery-notebook world is a welcoming one.

It is heartening to "meet"—even online—others of our kind because most pencil people are the Tigger in their circle of friends: they are the only ones. Even when we gather, we don't usually constitute a crowd. For the most part, the people in the pencil world are enablers, often pushing people to use the good China or applauding someone for having sharpened a rare pencil that could fetch sixty dollars on eBay.

The good news is that there really aren't non-pencil people and I have never met anyone who could be considered anti-pencil. (Until I worked on this project, I had never met anyone who admitted to having even an aversion to pencils.) Most people use pencils, even if it's just once in a while, like when they fill out the lottery slip when the Powerball jackpot tops one billion dollars. The even better news is that pencils have a use beyond collecting. They are always functional—even the ninety-year-old pencil that I used while I was doing research in the Massachusetts Archives still writes as well as it did when it rolled out of the Brooklyn factory where it was made. (The eraser, however, has not withstood the test of time. It is toast.)

I have squirreled away some collectibles and have acquired far more pencils than I could use, even if I was a teacher in a third-grade classroom where pencils seemed to disappear during the school day. No, seriously, where do pencils go in third-grade classrooms? The students don't eat them (at least I think that's true), but the number of pencils in the "sharpened" and "to be sharpened" containers is always significantly smaller at the end of the day. My entire pencil collection could be put to work. I have seen schools in other parts of the world that would celebrate its arrival.

Okay, I'll admit, that is what we pencil people tell ourselves, that *all* of our collection is worthwhile and useful. But most people do have a pencil story. It is of a time when they were in school, took a test, stole a pencil from someone—or maybe stole a pencil from someone after losing their own to take a test—couldn't find a pencil, or found some in their grandfather's workshop in the basement. That last one is something that unites pencil collectors with just regular pencil-using folks: who can resist the pull of saving something that a now-gone but cherished relative used? We pencil collectors are not as showy as the automobile fanatics and, I'll admit, no pencil is as sexy as a 1965 Ford Mustang. But a pencil is a masterpiece of engineering and design, and I can carry around my most treasured pieces in a backpack. Ralph Lauren can't do that with his museum-worthy car collection. Some of his cars are *never* driven. To quote a pair of socks with images of books and pencils that one of my sisters gave me as a gift: "I'm a nerd, but not the cool kind."

So, how do we identify each other? Pencil people will engage others when they spot a "good" pencil in use—a Tombow Mono 100 or a Faber-Castell Grip Graphite Eco—because you don't find those brands in your local CVS. We seek out the stores, websites, and companies that sell and manufacture various pencils. We know the locations of stores that sell pencils, pens, inks, highlighters, envelopes, paper, notebooks, journals, and other stationery around where we live and in any city we have visited. When someone finds something and shares it online, expect that store to have a rush—okay, a noticeable uptick—of customers.

I cannot write of pencil stores or pencil people without noting the sadness I felt at the 2021 closing of Caroline Weaver's CW Pencil Enterprise, which was dedicated to all types of wood-case pencils and their immediate family:

erasers, sharpeners, pencil cases, and some notebooks. The first location at 100 Forsyth Street in New York City's Lower East Side was a narrow storefront that gave off an art gallery vibe with its white walls, clean shelves, and curated stock. It was in that location that I first found the contemporary Palomino Blackwing in the limited-edition "Volumes" series. I bought a box of the Volume 725 and a box of the 1138 upon their releases in 2015 for less than thirty dollars each. (A full box of twelve pencils of either model would fetch at least ten times that in 2023. And, yes, I kick myself for not buying an extra box of each.) The 725 was made as a tribute to the Newport Folk Festival and takes its bright sunburst of red and yellow from the design of a Fender Stratocaster guitar. The 1138 took its theme from the Georges Méliès film *A Trip to the Moon*, that has 1138 frames, which create the pencil's design of black, white, and gray stripes. The themes for each are explained on the company's website and the boxes for each release, but you don't have to know the backstory to appreciate a particular pencil.

I met California Cedar Products Company CEO Charles Berolzheimer at CW Pencil's second location, at 15 Orchard Street not far from the original site, where he signed a copy of a book on his family's company. (He inscribed my copy using an Eberhard Faber Blu-Blak Noblot 740, which leaves an indelible mark.) I met some fellow pencil lovers in person that day after becoming familiar with them from online forums for a while. Yet Weaver's store was not about Blackwing, modern or vintage, for me. It was where I could find new pencils from

Japan, India, and Portugal, along with European brands that offered a range of pencils for every job and function.

When Weaver closed her shop after seven years, the community felt its loss but was buoyed by the number of other shops that had followed her path. In my part of the world, Massachusetts, we have many: The Boston General Store in Brookline sells pencil samplers so that buyers can try several brands, pulled together by type, and in West Newton, the Paper Mouse stocks writing instruments, notebooks, and their own Felix Doolittle brand cards and prints by co-owner and artist Felix Fu. In Cambridge, there are University Stationery Co. and Bob Slate Stationer, the latter of which is a regular at the annual Commonwealth Pen Show, which lets we pencil people come and play.

Another local shop that caterers to the community at-large is Calliope Paperie in Natick, where owner Kristina Burkey has a store full of stickers and pencils and pens and cards and Washi tape, and stationery items too numerous to name. (The Main Street store also has a Ms. Pac-Man arcade game.) In 2022, Burkey started Stationery Store Day on the first Saturday of August to celebrate those brick-and-mortar stores that sell stationery, of course, but also cater to those who buy it. I was there on that hot, sunny Saturday morning, arriving within the first hour Calliope was open. As I walked under the sign with its big yellow pencil border and into the store, I found it packed with happy people picking out their purchases. The scene would play out in several stores a short ride from Natick and to locations around the United States.

Pencil lovers must be an actual community because we have holidays. National Pencil Day has been celebrated on March 30 since the 1970s because it was on that day that Hymen Lipman, a Philadelphia entrepreneur, received a patent for his invention of inserting an eraser into wood-case pencils. It was considered revolutionary as pencils and erasers had previously always been sold separately. World Stationery Day is recognized annually on the last Wednesday of April and usually prompts a few stories on television news broadcasts, and there is also a National Stationery Day.

Fans of pencils, notebooks, and other pencil-adjacent things who do not have access to so many shops and supplies find other ways like online forums, Facebook groups, Reddit threads, and in-person events. You'll find pencil people at the various pen shows that are held each year around the world, which is a fun place to catch up on all things pen and a true playground if you are a mechanical pencil person. In 2019, I traveled to London for work, and my trip overlapped with the London Pen Show. It was a great chance to meet some people I had interacted with online, who introduced me to many people including the team from Makers Cabinet, the makers of the Høvel, a high-end pencil sharpener that works like a tiny wood plane. (Before you can even formulate the question, yes, of course, I bought one from them.) It was on that trip that I made my first visit to the stationery store Present & Correct, which I learned about by posting a notice that I was going to be in a town and was looking for shopping recommendations (a typical post to make in the community).

I have since made several purchases online from that sublime store and had them shipped from London to my house.

This community of pencil friends and others like it for fans of typewriters, typewriter ribbon tins, books, Little Free Library stewards, ephemera, and Field Notes notebooks all helped me get through the Covid-19 shutdown, particularly the first months of isolation in 2020. I participated in Zoom "meetups," did trades on social media, and watched live author events. One of the more interesting things was a live online tour offered by the magazine and travel company Atlas Obscura of Jaina Bee's *Granny's Empire of Art* home in San Francisco that is decorated throughout and features wall installations made from more than 185,000 colored and graphite pencils. There were pencils affixed to doors, walls, stairs, and furniture.

Somehow the world was made smaller and my own daily life a little bigger by these interactions with others. Writing, journaling, using pencils and pens, and more deliberate methods of getting thoughts together were also ways through those uncertain times. It was a bright and comforting space for me. People freely sent postcards, pencil "care packages," sticker swaps, typewritten letters, and packs of notebooks. I did not think that there could be a dark side to such interactions but it, too, happened during the pandemic.

In the days after a Black man named George Floyd was killed on May 25, 2020, by a white police officer in Minneapolis, Minnesota, the outrage felt by so many spilled into the streets in the form of protests and riots throughout the United States. In response, many stationery manufacturers and stores joined other national companies in raising money to support various community organizations. One person in a Facebook group that I belong to took exception. "I prefer my pencils to be apolitical," the person wrote. My heart sank. How did pencils and the people using them become political at all? But I was buoyed by a quick and thoughtful response in opposition—there aren't two sides to everything, certainly not racism. The group's administrators reaffirmed the community's standards and after a few other adjustments, the group's members raised even more money than expected for worthy causes. I saw similar incidents play out in different groups and on various platforms in that early part of the summer of 2020.

The initial reaction caught me off-guard because many of these groups and others like them on more freewheeling platforms had, for the most part, an air of comity and respect. Upon further reflection, however, I realized that I had left threads, chats, and groups (or started participating less in them) that had attitudes of exclusivity or secret knowledge, but I had not been deliberate in my choices until the aftermath of the George Floyd protests. I hope to never make that mistake again and am thankful to have found some places that feel worthy of my time. I also realized that pencil collecting had been a hobby that primarily skewed male, White, and to the Midwestern United States, but that, thankfully, is changing.

For me, pencils are uniters. The world of pencils overlaps with other interests like books, pens, letterpress and printing, music and vinyl records, tattooing, visual arts, typewriters, notebooks, and journaling. I have met people, gotten to know about them, their backgrounds and families, and learned about different parts of the country all through the pencils I collected from others. There is no real hierarchy except for those people who brag about doing the *New York Times* crossword puzzle in ink and think they are superior. (Okay, maybe the people who sketch or journal every day or make significant progress in their To Be Read pile deserve to feel superior.) I do the *Times* mini crossword on my cell phone because it's just so darn convenient.

Pencils are the most object-y of objects. There is no learning curve for use. No training is involved. In a world where there are directions for use on everything, pencils (thankfully, and at least at the time this book is going to press) do not come with the instructions: Take a pencil out of the box. Sharpen. Write. Draw. Create. Repeat.

Some might want to write the pencil's obituary, probably on their cell phones, as others have when the ballpoint pen was first mass produced or the typewriter gave way to word processors and, later, personal computers of all sizes. I, however, am giving the pencil its commencement address, a celebratory note to mark centuries of its use. I know that the pencil's life begins anew as each one is picked out and put to task to create and, in the best cases, to be used until it doesn't have anything left to give.

AFTERWORD

This book is late. That is not something that someone who worked in daily news for many years should ever write, but the first rule of journalism is to tell the truth. And that first sentence is the truth. The larger reality is that one might never really be finished with a project about something they love or an object they have spent so much time thinking about, discussing, and collecting. In this case, it wasn't laziness or hubris but life that got in the way: Life, health, and the world such as it is in 2023.

After I apologized to the teams at Object Lessons and Bloomsbury for how I missed that deadline, I started thinking about how I got past that and completed this project. The answer is the basics, using the pencils and pens and paper and notebooks that I had always relied on to start again and work through things. I could think again, with the help of pencil and paper. As I wrote in the opening pages of this book, the pencil requires you to pick it up, hold it and sharpen it. It enlivens all the senses. Pencils (and the related objects in my kit) got me back in full working order. I owe the pencil some gratitude in addition to the appreciation I already had.

In the last few years, I, like so many others, have had to ensure that I used available technology to support my humanity. A telehealth call with my doctor to avoid a waiting room? Perfect. But believe me, I was always taking notes by hand during those visits.

This time has brought to mind something that the artist Vincent van Gogh wrote on September 24, 1880, to his younger brother Theo, an art dealer. "I shall get over it somehow, I shall set to work again with my pencil, which I cast aside in my deep dejection, and I shall draw again . . . and now I am in my stride and my pencil has become slightly more willing and it seems to be getting more so by the day."[1] I love the quote, not so much for the melodrama of the discouragement, but for the artist assigning the willingness of renewed inspiration to his pencil.

I also thought about how I came to the Object Lessons project. I was at a book reading for Henry Louis Gates, Jr., at the Harvard Book Store a few years ago and spotted the series titles lined up along a shelf. Two caught my eye, *Tumor* and *Tree*, and I was fascinated from the first pages. Matthew Battles writes in *Tree* about the towering species in the Arnold Arboretum, a park of a sort in Boston managed by Harvard University but miles away from its campus, that I make a point to visit at least once a year. It hit home.

Rereading Battles's *Tree* in 2022, I was acutely aware of how trees were so much a part of my life. Not just the actual trees Battles wrote of, but all trees—their wood and shade, their fruit and nuts, their very presence in my yard. I also caught my breath and hoped that the tree worshippers are wrong about these plants. Because if the trees ever figure out how many of their kind that I have killed in the name of putting out newspapers, making pencils, or publishing books, I will not be safe walking down the streets of Boston or New York.

I say cheers to those who sharpen their pencils with a knife to make it just *so* and to those who seek out the perfect paper to write on—and to you for going on this journey.

ACKNOWLEDGMENTS

This book is the result of years of thinking about pencils, talking about pencils and collecting pencils. I need to thank all of those in my life who have indulged me in this, particularly Mom, Terry and Joe, Patty, Mickey and Margie, Matthew, Mike and Martina, Patrick, Bridget, Colm and Brogan Donston. There are many relatives to thank from the Beggy, O'Bryan, Gallagher, Bruner, Garrison, and Waite wings of the family, and there are the Camp, Edgewood, Arlington, Pittsburgh, and St. Anselm branches that have been my "family" for generations now.

This book would not be possible without the help of Gary Salt, Doug Martin, Andrew Westberg, Dave Tubman, Jim Concannon, Julia Spitz, Eileen McGill, Bruce and Susan Wheltle, Nicole and Tim Delger, John Spooner, Zack Bond, Ed Kemp, the Concord Public Library, the Boston Public Library, the members of the American Pencil Collectors Society, the participants of the Erasable Podcast Pencil Community, the RSVP Stationery and the Collecting Vintage Pencils and Pencil Sharpeners Facebook groups, and the other unnamed collectors who came before me, those who believed that each pencil can be magical.

A special note of gratitude for the patience and guidance of Haaris Naqvi and Rachel Moore at Bloomsbury Publishing, and the vision of the Object Lessons team, specifically Ian Bogost and Christopher Schaberg.

There are many friends, colleagues, and extended family that have supported me in this and so many of my projects (and gifted me pencils and sent postcards from their far-flung travels). Their kindness can never be fully repaid, but I will say thank you here: Bill and Ginnie Brett, Jan Saragoni and Frank Phillips, Jayne Larson and Darrell Blocker, Robyn Holloway and Mary Lou Cavanaugh, Michela Larson and Ed Marino, Francesca Nadalini, George Larson, Chris Haynes, Stephanie Callahan, Sal Scamardo and Eric Turner, Terri Stanley, John McDermott, Jim Fahey, Stan Meyer, Annemarie Lewis Kerwin and Mark Kerwin, Tony Corey, Drew Holt, Heather White, Melanie Platten, Heloise Borden, Desi Gonzalez, Travis Vautour, Anthony Jarvis, Bryan Margaca, Jason Margaca, James Costa and John Archibald, Diane Borger, Fiona Sinclair, Mike Sereda, Bob Tremblay, Naomi Kooker, Kevin Fennessy, Joanne Barrett, Mary Cannetti, Gayle Jones, Meg Harris, Melissa Carr and Jess Chloros and sons, Nikos and Jack, the Porfidos, the McAllisters, Jack Doherty, Joe Bradlee, Anna Bradlee, Cassandra Henderson, Karen Johansen and Gardner Hendrie, Jim Fagan, Elaine Driscoll, Robert Knott, Elaine Delaney, Barbara Meltz, Tim Stansky, Fred Balboni, his mom, Emma, and their whole crew, Sarah

Pennell, Kristin Allison, Mary Gallant, Peggy Jeram, Aimee Kerr, Ashley Bernon & Co., Barry Miller, Sherrie Johnson, Diane Quinn, Georgia Lyman, Michele McPhee, Jonathan Tucker, Maggie Moss-Tucker, Wendy Pierce, Donna Eden Cohen, Dick Flavin, the Cafarellis, Karen Porter, Dorothy Williams, Guthrie Taylor, Rachel Warner, Ashley Weaver, Colleen Turner and Tom Secino, Vanessa Parks, Tom Mulvoy, Ed Forry, Denise Pons Leone, and my friends at Staples Studio, Store No. 1.

NOTES

Introduction

1 "King Charles loses his temper at leaking pen: 'Every stinking time'" (video story), *The Independent*, September 13, 2022, https://www.youtube.com/watch?v=oUWcyqOm8AY.

2 Petroski, Henry, *The Pencil: A History of Design and Circumstances* (New York: Knopf, 1992), xi.

3 Kemp, Ellie and Steven Smith, "Why we use pencils when we vote in elections: You can bring a pen, though," *WalesOnline*, May 5, 2022. https://www.walesonline.co.uk/news/uk-news/use-pencils-vote-elections-23868950.

4 Whitman, Sarah, "Is Dixon's Ticonderoga Truly 'The World's Best Pencil'? We Don't Think So.'" *Wirecutter*, (blog). *New York Times,* October 15, 2022. https://www.nytimes.com/wirecutter/blog/dixon-ticonderoga-pencil/.

5 Pencils.com (blog), "John Steinbeck: the Ultimate Pencil Pusher," March 2016. https://blog.pencils.com/john-steinbeck-the-ultimate-pencil-pusher/.

Chapter 1

1 Betty Cornfield and Owen Edwards, *Quintessence: The Quality of Having It* (New York: Crown Publishers, 1983).

2 Hilary Mantel, "The joys of stationery." *The Guardian*, March 5, 2010.
https://www.theguardian.com/books/2010/mar/06/hilary
-mantel-stationery-writers-notebook.

3 *New York Times*, "Lou Brooks Obituary, 1944-2021, Lou Brooks, Ground-breaking Creative, dies at 77," December 21, 2021.https://www.legacy.com/us/obituaries/nytimes/
name/lou-brooks-obituary?id=31964714.

4 The Museum of Forgotten Art Supplies, https://www.forgott
enartsupplies.com/.

5 "Creativity for Life: Graphite Pencil Lead Degree Hardness," Faber-Castell, https://www.fabercastell.com/blogs/creativity
-for-life/graphite-pencil-lead-degree-hardness#.

6 Pencils.com (blog), "The History of the Bullet Pencil," https://blog.pencils.com/the-history-of-the-bullet-pencil/.

7 *Webster's Collegiate Dictionary*, fifth edition, (Springfield, Mass.: MG.&C. Merriam Co., 1948), 733.

Chapter 2

1 Christopher Payne and Sam Anderson, "Inside One of America's Last Pencil Factories: A photographer captures a colorful world of craft and complexity." *New York Times Magazine*, January 12, 2018. https://www.nytimes.com/2018

/01/12/magazine/inside-one-of-americas-last-pencil-factories
.html.

2 General Pencil Company website, "Our History." https://www
.generalpencil.com/history.html.

3 The Pencil Pages, "J.R. Moon Pencil Company." http://www
.pencilpages.com/mfg/jrmoon.htm.

4 Musgrave Pencil Company website, "Our Company History."
https://musgravepencil.com/pages/history-musgrave-custom
-pencils.

5 "Dixon Crucible Company." *Jersey City Past and Present*
(blog). New Jersey City University. August 21, 2021. https://
njcu.libguides.com/dixon.

6 Paletta, Damian, "How Dixon Ticonderoga has blurred lines
of where its pencils are made." *Washington Post*, September
26, 2018. https://www.washingtonpost.com/business/
economy/how-dixon-ticonderoga-has-blurred-lines-of-where
-its-pencils-are-made/2018/09/19/0e9be518-b207-11e8-9a6a
-565d92a3585d_story.html.

7 "Blackwing 602," *Wikipedia*, updated April 2, 2023. https://en
.wikipedia.org/wiki/Blackwing_602.

8 *Atlanta Constitution* advertisement, October 18, 1918, 4.

9 William Ecenbarger, "What's portable, chewable, doesn't leak
and is recommended by Ann Landers? Pencils are amazing
things, and the ones made in Pennsylvania by Eberhard Faber
may be the best in the world." *Philadelphia Inquirer*, June 16,
1985, 14.

10 Ibid.

11 *Cawker City Public Record*, December 23, 1886, 6.

12 "Pencil." *Made up in Britian* (blog) https://madeupinbritain.uk
/Pencil.

13 "The Wad Mines worth a King's Ransom." *Lakestay* (blog) http://www.lakestay.co.uk/wad.htm.

14 Ryan Kellman, Elissa Nadworny, and Adam Cole, "Trace The Remarkable History Of The Humble Pencil." *All Things Considered, NPR*, October 11, 2016. https://www.npr.org/sections/ed/2016/10/11/492999969/origin-of-pencil-lead.

Chapter 3

1 *The Gentleman of the World, the Entertaining Magazine*, 1771. Held in the internal electronic archives of the Boston Public Library, property of the National Library of Ireland.

2 "Milwaukee Pencil Dater." *Wisconsin Library Heritage Center* (blog), https://heritage.wisconsinlibraries.org/entry/milwaukee-pencil-dater/.

3 William Ecenbarger. "A Case in Point: More than 200 years after its invention, the pencil is still something to write home about." *Baltimore Sun*, July 14, 1991. https://www.baltimoresun.com/news/bs-xpm-1991-07-14-1991195196-story.html.

Chapter 4

1 Huston, Caitlin, "Sondheim During 2022 Tony Awards: 'Company' won a number of awards, including best musical revival, on Sunday, prompting further remembrances." *Hollywood Reporter*, June 12, 2022. https://www.hollywoodreporter.com/lifestyle/arts/stephen-sondheim-tribute-tony-awards-2022-1235164088/.

2 Max, D.T., "Stephen Sondheim's Lesson for Every Artist."
New Yorker, February 14, 2022. https://www.newyorker.com
/culture/the-new-yorker-interview/stephen-sondheim-final
-interviews.

3 Leddy, Michael. "Stephen Sondheim on pencils, paper."
Orange Crate Art (blog). May 10, 2010. https://mleddy
.blogspot.com/2010/05/stephen-sondheim-on-pencils-and
-paper.html.

4 Mosendz, Polly. "This 25-year-old is Turning a Profit Selling
Pencils." *Bloomberg*, April 12, 2016. https://www.bloomberg
.com/news/articles/2016-04-12/this-25-year-old-is-turning-a
-profit-selling-pencils.

5 Abramovitch, Seth. "Why Is Hollywood Obsessed With This
Pencil? The Blackwing 602 went out of production in 1998;
now, on its 80th birthday, everyone from Stephen Sondheim
to 'Mad Men' to top studio animators have made it one of
the industry's most valuable—and quickly disappearing—
possessions." *Hollywood Reporter*, August 16, 2013. https://
www.hollywoodreporter.com/gallery/7-cult-objects-top
-screenwriters-602818/1-stephen-sondheim-and-the
-blackwing-602/.

6 O'Neill, Eugene, *Exorcism, A Play in One Act*, (Hartford,
Conn., Yale University Press, 2012), 10. https://books.google
.com/books?id=gV2Hou1bPiIC&q=Eugene+O%27Neill
%2BBlackwing+pencil&pg=PP10.

7 Laurents, Arthur, *Original Story by: A Memoir of
Broadway and Hollywood* (New York: Hal Leonard
Corporation, 2001), 5.

8 Riddle, Nelson, *Arranged by Nelson Riddle* (Van Nuys,
California: Alfred Music Publishing, 1985).

9   White, Martha, ed., *E.B. White: Quotations from America's Most Companionable of Writers* (Ithaca, N.Y.: Cornell University Press, 2011), 1.

10 Christie, Marian. "Francoise and Oscar fool the prophets of doom: When the fashion powers merge." *Boston Globe*, October 19, 1969, A9.

11 The conversation took place while I worked as a student at *The Boston Globe* when Marian Christy came into the newsroom. While there she asked for some help in gathering "clips" from the newspaper's library and supplies, which were all analog.

12 Raab Collection Auction Catalog, https://www.raabcollection.com/john-williams-autograph/john-williams-signed-sold-pencil-wrote-most-famous-score-movie-history-star.

13 Ernest Hemingway and Sean Hemingway, ed., *A Moveable Feast: The Restored Edition.* (New York: Scribner's.), 169.

14 Benchley, Nathaniel, "John Steinbeck, The Art of Fiction No. 45," *Paris Review*, Issue 48, Fall 1969.

15 Ibid.

16 Ibid.

17 Bauman Rare Books, auction catalog, https://www.baumanrarebooks.com/rare-books/edison-thomas-alva/autograph-letter-signed/71299.aspx.

18 Petroski, Henry, *The Pencil: A History of Design and Circumstances* (New York: Knopf, 1992), 22-23.

19 Ecenbarger, William, "What's portable . . ." 18.

20 "In Lincoln's Hand." Remembering Lincoln at Gettysburg (blog). Cornell University. 2103. https://rmc.library.cornell.edu/gettysburg150/exhibition/lincolnshand/index.html.

21 William Ecenbarger, "What's portable . . ." 18.

Chapter 5

1   "Space Pens, Pencils, and How NASA Takes Notes in Space: The real story behind the iconic Space Pen and how NASA testing helped it soar." *Spinoff* (blog). NASA. August 27, 2021. https://spinoff.nasa.gov/space-pens#.

2   Ibid.

3   *The West Wing*, "We Killed Yamamoto" Season 3, Episode 21, first aired May 15, 2002, written by Aaron Sorkin.

4   *Spinoff*, "Space Pens, Pencils, and How NASA Takes Notes in Space."

5   "Pencil; Hoover for President 1928," Smithsonian Institution, https://collections.si.edu/search/detail/edanmdm:nasm_A19410007007

6   Ibid.

7   "Mechanical Pencil, Shuttle," Smithsonian Institution, https://collections.si.edu/search/detail/edanmdm:nasm_A20130275000

8   Horrigan, Sharon, "American Classic." *Opportunity*, Spring 2018, 11.

    https://www.nib.org/wp-content/uploads/2019/02/NIB_OppMagazine_Spring_2018_WEB_508-1.pdf#page=11.

9   Cision, "National Industries for the Blind Celebrates 50th Anniversary of SKILCRAFT U.S. Government Pen: Iconic product symbolizes capabilities of people who are blind." April 24, 2018. https://www.prnewswire.com/news-releases/national-industries-for-the-blind-celebrates-50th-anniversary-of-skilcraft-us-government-pen-300635393.html?tc=eml_cleartime.

10 Federal Trade Commission Decisions, "Findings, Orders, and Stipulations," Volume 46, July 1, 1949, to June 30, 1950, 1242.

Chapter 6

1 Karolczak, Jessica, "Pencils unite collectors across the U.S. in Sioux Center." *nwestiowa.com*, June 19, 2017. https://www.nwestiowa.com/obituaries/ronald-brink-75-orange-city/article_4300fc3e-180b-11e9-a8bc-332f4b3af623.html.

2 Auction for the Thoreau Society, March 31, 2023. https://www.biddingforgood.com/auction/item/item.action?id=342705086.

3 The Ice Creamers, https://www.icescreamers.com/.

Chapter 7

1 Dussault, Mike, "Cutting off the Sleeves: The History of Bill Belichick and His Hoodie." *Bleacher Report*, June 14, 2013. https://bleacherreport.com/articles/1668165-cutting-off-the-sleeves-the-history-of-bill-belichick-and-his-hoodie.

2 Bergun, David, "M*A*S*H's Alan Alda Was an Army Officer in Korean and Played One on TV, *DOD News*, December 15, 2021. https://www.defense.gov/News/Feature-Stories/Story/Article/2866032/mashs-alan-alda-was-an-army-officer-in-korea-and-played-one-on-tv/.

3 Barber, James, "Alan Alda Asked AI to Write a New 'M*A*S*H' Scene in 2023," *Military.com*, March 9, 2023. https://www

.military.com/off-duty/television/2023/03/09/alan-alda-asked
-ai-write-new-mash-scene-2023.html.

4   Aly, Setphanie, "The stories behind everything on Seth Meyers'
    Late Night desk," *latenightest*, June 29, 2022. https://latenightist
    .com/history/the-stories-behind-everything-on-seth-meyers
    -late-night-desk/.

5   *John Wick*, released by Summit Entertainment/Lions Gate,
    2014, written by Derek Kolstad.

6   Chan, Ilsa, "Staedtler Pencil, Which Was Used As Weapon In
    The Glory, Sold Out In Korea Thanks To The Song Hye Kyo
    Drama: The humble pencil has become an unlikely fashion
    accessory." *8Days*, March 26, 2023. https://www.8days.sg/
    entertainment/asian/glory-staedtler-pencil-sold-out-763691.

7   Hirshberg, Lynn, "Danielle Deadwyler is Tár Director
    Todd Field's New Muse: For *W*'s Directors Issue, Field cast
    the *Till* star in 'What's Underneath,' a photo essay inspired by
    his favorite film noirs." *W Magazine*, February 28, 2023. https://
    www.wmagazine.com/culture/danielle-deadwyler-todd-field
    -tar-directors-issue-cover.

8   HC 101H: The Pencil, course description, University of
    Oregon, Professor Daniel Rosenberg.

9   Ibid.

Chapter 8

1   Petroski, Henry, *The Pencil: A History of Design and
    Circumstances* (New York: Knopf, 1992), 3-4.

2   Wood, David F., *An Observant Eye: The Thoreau Collection at
    the Concord Museum* (Concord, Mass.: Concord Museum,
    2006), 85.

3   Thoreau, Henry David, The Project Gutenberg eBook of *Walden; or, Life in the Woods*. https://www.gutenberg.org/files/205/205-h/205-h.htm.

4   Fedorko, Kathy, "Henry's Brilliant Sister: The Pivotal Role of Sophia Thoreau in Her Brother's Posthumous Publications." *New England Quarterly*, May 23, 2016.

5   Goodman, Russell B., *Stanford Encyclopedia of Philosophy Online* revised August 30, 2019. https://plato.stanford.edu/entries/transcendentalism/.

6   Alcott, Louisa May "Thoreau's Flute: A Poem." *Atlantic Monthly*, September 1863, 280-281. https://www.theatlantic.com/magazine/archive/1863/09/thoreaus-flute/540804/.

7   "The Timeless Sculpture of Daniel Chester French," *Antiques & Fine Art Magazine*, Autumn/Winter 2013. https://www.incollect.com/articles/a-heritage-of-beauty.

8   "The Minute Man Statue by Daniel Chester French." National Park Service (blog). https://www.nps.gov/mima/learn/historyculture/the-minute-man-statue-by-daniel-chester-french.htm.

9   Wood, 86.

10 Ibid., 85.

11 Petroski, 101.

12 "Early American Pencils." *Acton Trails* (blog), June 25, 2009. https://web.archive.org/web/20090625130359/http://www.actontrails.org/EAPencils.htm.

13 Wood, 87.

14 Harvard College, Class of 1837 notes 10th anniversary, 1847. https://hollisarchives.lib.harvard.edu/repositories/4/resources/4172.

15 John Kaag, "Me for the Woods." *Paris Review*, June 30. 2017. https://www.theparisreview.org/blog/2017/06/30/me-for-the-woods/.

16 Ibid.

Chapter 9

1 Saul, Stephanie. "Put Down Your No. 2 Pencils. Forever.: The SAT will go completely digital by 2024 amid questions about whether college admissions tests are fair, or even necessary." *New York Times,* January 25, 2022. https://www.nytimes.com/2022/01/25/us/sat-test-digital.html.

2 *Merriam-Webster's Collegiate Dictionary*, 11th edition, (Springfield, MA: Merriam-Webster, Inc., August 1, 2019), https://www.merriam-webster.com/dictionary/skeuomorph.

3 Holtermann, Callie, "When a Sharpened Pencil Just Isn't Enough: Nonprofit groups bolster educational pursuits by helping young people get the little things — a printer, a book that inspires — that make a big difference." *New York Times*, October 20, 2022. https://www.nytimes.com/2022/10/20/neediest-cases/when-a-sharpened-pencil-just-isnt-enough.html.

Afterword

1 Vincent van Gogh, letter to his brother Theo on September 24, 1880. Translation by Johanna van Gogh-Bonger, edited by Robert Harrison. https://www.webexhibits.org//vangogh/letter/8/136.htm.

SELECTED BIBLIOGRAPHY AND SUGGESTED FURTHER READING

Baker, Samantha Dion. *Draw Your World: How to Sketch and Paint Your Remarkable Life*. New York: Watson-Guptill, 2021.

Berolzheimer, Charles P. II. *The Story of Cal Cedar: 100 Years of Pencil Supply History*. California: Blackwing Press, 2017.

Coelho, Paulo. *Like a Flowing River, The Story of the Pencil*. New York: HarperCollins, 2007.

Cornfield, Betty and Owen Edwards. *Quintessence: The Quality of Having It*. New York: Crown Publishers, 1983.

Gross, Robert A. *The Transcendentalists and Their World*. New York: Farrar, Straus and Giroux, 2021.

Hammond, Alex and Mike Tinney. *The Secret Life of the Pencil: Great Creatives and Their Pencils*. London: Laurence King Publishing, 2017.

Mattes, Mark Alan, ed. *Handwriting in Early America: A Media History*. Amherst: University of Massachusetts Press, 2023.

Pepperell, Keith. *The Lead in Your Pencil: A History of Pencil Hardness*. CreateSpace Independent Publishing Platform, 2015.

Petroski, Henry. *The Pencil: A History of Design and Circumstance*. New York: Knopf, 1990.

Rees, David. *How to Sharpen Pencils: A Practical & Theoretical Treatise on the Artisanal Craft of Pencil Sharpening for Writers, Artists, Contractors, Flange Turners, Anglesmiths, & Civil Servants*. New York: Melville House Books, 2012.

Veley, Jonathan A. *A Century of Autopoint*. Ohio: Legendary Lead Company, 2019.

Veley, Jonathan A. *The Leadhead's Pencil Blog*, Vols. 1–7. Ohio: Legendary Lead Company, 2012–2019.

Weaver, Caroline. *The Pencil Perfect: The Untold Story of a Cultural Icon*. Berlin: Gestalten, 2107.

Weaver, Caroline. *Pencils You Should Know: A History of the Ultimate Utensil in 75 Anecdotes*. San Francisco: Chronicle Books, 2020.

Wood, David F. *An Observant Eye: The Thoreau Collection at the Concord Museum*. Concord: Concord Museum, 2006.

Websites and blogs

American Pencil Collectors Society, http://www.pencilcollector.org/

Blackwing Pages, https://blackwingpages.com/ and https://blackwingpages.wordpress.com/

Brand Name Pencils, https://brandnamepencils.com/

Fred's Pencils, https://fredspencils.wordpress.com/

Led Fast, https://www.leadfast.org/

Pencils, eh, https://pencilseh.weebly.com/

Pencil Fodder, https://pencilfodder.com/

Pencil Talk, https://www.penciltalk.org/

Polar Pencil Pusher, https://polarpencilpusher.home.blog/
The Pencil Pages, http://www.pencilpages.com/
Well-appointed desk, https://www.wellappointeddesk.com
Woodclinched, https://woodclinched.com/

Podcasts

Erasable Podcast, https://www.erasable.us/
RSVP: A podcast about stationery and so much more, https://rsv
    pstationerypodcast.com/
The Pen Addict, https://www.penaddict.com/
Sharpened Artist, Colored Pencil Podcast, https://sharpenedartist
    .com/podcast

Publications and Zines

Fountain Pen Journal, http://www.fountainpenjournal.com/
Pencil of the Week, edited by Ed Kemp, https://www.etsy.com/shop
    /TheWordDistribution
Pencil Revolution, edited by Johnny Gamber, https://
    pencilrevolution.com/
Note: By design Zines are limited run publications, so the two
    sites listed above may not have all issues. A good general site
    for a variety of Zines is Antiquated Future, which usually
    has *Pencil of the Week* and *Pencil Revolution*, https://www
    .antiquatedfuture.com/.

Pencil videos and documentaries

No. 2, The Story of the Pencil, a 2015 documentary written and directed by William Allen that features a number of people mentioned in this book as well as others.

Why the Pencil is Perfect, Caroline Weaver's TED Talk, part of the Small Thing Big Idea series that had been viewed more than 1.4 million times as this book was going to press, https://www.ted.com/talks/caroline_weaver_why_the_pencil_is_perfect.

I, Pencil, Milton Friedman's talk, https://www.youtube.com/watch?v=67tHtpac5ws.

How Erasers Are Made, on the Insider channel, more than 10 million views, https://www.youtube.com/watch?v=lRrWZVtibXw.

How We Make Pencils, Faber-Castell, https://www.youtube.com/watch?v=aPb-slJH9Vs.

The Always Analog YouTube Channel, https://www.youtube.com/@AlwaysAnalog.

INDEX